ONE LAST MIRACLE

ONE LAST MIRACLE

André Martineau

VANTAGE PRESS
New York

Cover photograph by Claudette Davis (1967),
photogaphed by Marc Paradis.

This novel was translated by Brian W. Fisher and André Martineau

FIRST EDITION

Copyright © 2003 by André Martineau
Published by Vantage Press, Inc.
516 West 34th Street, New York, New York 10001

Manufactured in the United States of America
ISBN: 0-533-14563-5

Library of Congress Catalog Card No. 2003091625

0 9 8 7 6 5 4 3 2 1

To my mother
and
To Claudette

After thirty-five years of sobriety, the author has left his anonymity with the only purpose of giving hope to those who have lost their confidence in life.

Respecting the tradition of Alcoholics Anonymous, the author of this book will only speak for himself and not as a member of A.A.

Contents

ONE LAST MIRACLE

Prologue

Life is not intended to lead to despair. . . . However, countless individuals continue to sign on to a wandering existence devoid of meaning. Many try to escape into alcohol and drugs. Others descend into madness or suicide.

But there is a path that leads to the fulfillment of every life: it is a faith in a Higher Power, which leads to a spiritual practice in which the soul and the mind are at peace, if we can only undertake it in complete humility.

To all those who despair, the following life story leaves no doubt as to the mysterious power of faith. The great despair of loneliness has been replaced by fulfillment and a serenity—leading to the wonderful discovery of kindred spirits and, often, to a sacred reunion with one's twin soul.

Yes, miracles of faith are real. . . . I am the living and incontestable proof.

1

False Starts

The downy flakes of spring snow danced to the sound of the church bells of Saint-Pierre-Claver in Montréal and a new life began: André was baptized on March 12th 1930 in the depths of the Depression. At the top of one of its pages, with accompanying photographs, the newspaper *La Presse* announced a fourth generation.

What a raucous beginning! Like any first child of a fourth generation, he drew forth the adoration of grandparents, and he was coaxed and loved by numerous aunts and uncles who actually fought each other to hold him. André was beautiful, well-mannered, gentle, sweet and intelligent, as everyone told him with constant flattery and adulation. The seed of pride was sown in the mind's fertile ground of this sensitive child, both emotional and at the same time naive enough to believe all those compliments. From the age of two, André, with his angelic honey-blond hair and warm brown velvet eyes, held serious conversations with adults. He was already a major contender for first place in this great family!

Four years of sweet indulgence went by before the arrival of his little brother, Pierre. André was not even jealous because he was still able to grab all the attention, and he knew from the start that he was better than his brother and all his other cousins coming after him. As time went by he believed himself to be already well ahead of the rest... evil had taken root and the monstrous demands of pride had started to affect his attitude and behaviour. It gradually began to destroy his life in all its aspects. This growing cancer was fed and encouraged by those close to him who didn't have the slightest suspicion of its underhandedness, the solicitude paving the way for the first false starts in his life.

Then the day came for André to leave his protective cocoon to enter the world outside and go into a competitive universe for which he was not prepared, since he had almost always stayed within the warm womb of his family. He was enrolled at l'Académie Saint-Germain in Outremont where he became the darling of the good sisters and brothers because he was so well-behaved, obedient, well brought up and, every week, every month and every year leading to his elementary school diploma, he was always first in his class. Besides, proud André would certainly never have tolerated second place without a major tantrum. He had to be number one or he was nothing!

At home compliments continued to rain down; but André's father always demanded more: to be first in class with a 90 percent average was never enough. With intelligence like that he should always be within a whisker of 100 percent! Moreover his father thought that he did not excel enough in school sports. Other demands soon made themselves felt, and, in a very subtle way, parents, teachers as well as the parish priest revealed to André the great secret of his future vocation: he had been chosen by God to become one of His priests! This elect of God, this young one, guided despite himself toward a destiny that he had not chosen, this child who would soon lose his holy innocence, well yes, it was me!

In the utter purity of my childhood I could not prevent myself from being taken over by a deep piety and a blind faith in all of the Catholic religion that was taught to me. Eyes closed, hands clasped, trembling with near contemplative emotion, I became a model altar boy at the age of seven, and I already knew by heart the necessary Latin to

4

respond to the presiding priest within the rigid frame of the liturgy of the time. Gifted with memory and a rare capacity for vocal projection, I was already happy to be the best server of mass in the whole school. Always first, still first, I progressed from simple altar boy to the position of acolyte, then to incense bearer and response leader, a little bit more and I would have insisted on replacing the priest!

Within the hierarchy of mass servers, the most important position is that of response leader, followed by incense bearer and at nine years of age, I refused to serve mass unless I was given one of these two assignments because the right to wear a white cassock with a red sash came with them.

This tainted pride invaded every corner of my young life, and I could never say yes to any setback, defeat, or second place. From the earliest days of my childhood, this self-imposed burden promised a coming life full of torment and indefinable stress. The lack of true awareness of my emotional and hypersensitive nature at the depths of my being had already damaged my soul. I was overcome by terrible fears in the face of my sins, hell, a vengeful God, death and war. I feared failure, my father's disapproval and his latent violence.

But my pride was still stronger than my fears. It repressed my nervousness and put my feelings to sleep whenever I was with other people; from then on, I had to hide to cry and to shudder, so that no one could uncover my weakness and my fear. This shell became my protection against the judgment of others, sheltered me from all my failings, and allowed me to save face. I even closed the door to my inner self and was unable to confide in the few friends that I had.

My three best friends were as emotional as I was and (obviously) shared my views on life: one of them, Michel, committed suicide at fourteen, the second, Sylvain, became a well-known poet and he too killed himself at the age of twenty-five or so, while the third, Claude, died at forty at the end of his vagrancy and misery. They say "birds of a feather flock together." But how then, did I outlive them? I was as unhappy as they were, if not more so. Naturally I should have taken the same road and disappeared like my best friends had done. But God wanted me to fail in my efforts at self-destruction because He reserved a very different fate for me.

At twelve, I still had no idea where babies came from, and my sexual education left me open to deviants who described mortal sins committed by certain kinds of men, with women performing all sorts of perverted games and other acts of degradation.

What horror! What blasphemy! What shamefulness! Each one of these revelations scandalized and revolted me. These sex stories were so dirty! At any rate, I could never believe that a baby could be born because of a mortal sin, and I never would dare to think that my father and mother would commit such immorality.

One day, I confided to my friends that we had a new little sister at home of whom I was very proud; one of those bad boys (who was eavesdropping) heard everything and said to me out loud in front of my friends that my father had f . . . d my mother and had committed a carnal sin, and that the result was my little sister! How sickening! In the blink of an eye, I lost all control. I lashed out at this monster and punched him in the mouth. My friends had a hard time stopping me, and the school yard monitor took me to the principal who sent me right home. I still have the scars on my right thumb from that little demon's teeth!

How then can I describe the immense pain, the unbearable suffering, the deep shame attached to this discovery? On the way home, I cried and I raged. I simply didn't understand anything. I couldn't accept the brutal reality that had invaded and destroyed forever my belief in the mysterious virgin birth and the source of Jesus and his angels. For

6

months my soul was filled with feelings of total disillusionment, revolt, and despair. I lied to my mother and invented an accident to explain my wounded thumb and my tears. Strangely enough, I did not want to avoid her, and it seemed that I loved her even more, as it was God who made her thus, then how could she be guilty? No, not my mother!

All in all, despite everything, I did have some wonderful times when I was young. After my gathering up all the medals and all the possible first places at school, the summer holidays would arrive. With them came the joy of rediscovering the countryside and the great outdoors of Saint-Placide, beside the Lac des-Deux-Montagnes,* at my grandfather and grandmother's cottage. For twelve weeks I would live surrounded by nature with its birds, flowers and small animals. I would have my all-white Peter Rabbit, my grass snakes, my toads, and my minnows in their summer aquarium. I went fishing with my grandfather who adored me and told me all of the lake's secrets that he had learned so long ago. He knew where every kind of fish was hiding and how to lure and hook them. For her part my grandmother knew how to prepare them along with all the other treats. That was the life, a loving family, the natural tranquility that surrounded us, the peace so longed for after all the emotional turmoil of a year at school.

Every summer came as a soothing balm that enabled me to recover my fragile emotional balance. I believe that those breaks allowed me to control my emotions and saved me from deep depression. The love of all my relatives permitted me to survive and to renew my hope and happiness for the future. My fears were temporarily calmed by the beauties of nature that wrapped me in the green quilt of its hills and the bright blue of its lake of unspoiled islands. But every fall brought me back to hard

*Lake of Two Mountains

reality. It was the return to Montréal, back to its noise and pollution, to that realm of sin, the land of the damned. There, once again, my pride had to rule to keep up this inescapable pretense and to hide my sickening sensitivity and weakness. For me it was a return to a kind of hell on earth. And each time, gloom and melancholy came back to overwhelm me in my solitude.

In the fall of 1942, I returned for my last year of elementary school. I was always first and best during the whole year, and I always came out on top in the final exams. But even if my report card said that I was first, the end of the year awards presentation was another story. I was sitting with my parents in the packed school assembly hall, and I got ready to accept first prize and to melt under the applause of the crowd! I could already hear the congratulations coming from everywhere, and my pride was doing quite well, thank you. The principal stood up and welcomed everyone before announcing the year's results. I was in a real state when it came time to name the top student, and I stood up at the same time as he began to proclaim in a loud voice: "The top student is Jacques G.!" My father quickly forced me back into my seat. I was in shock. This was inconceivable and totally unexpected. I didn't understand. My tears welled up, I felt sick to my stomach and my whole body was shaking.

"Second, André Martineau." My father pulled me upright and with one arm propelled me toward the principal who presented me with my diploma and my stack of awards. I was stunned and my pride was wounded to the quick. I felt totally dead inside on the trip home. My father was as angry as I was and demanded an explanation from the principal. The man finally admitted that he had buckled under pressure from his superiors to publicly honor Jacques G. with the top prize because he was the Lieutenant-Governor's grandson. He explained this away by saying that, after all, it didn't matter because my report card was proof that I really was the top student! From that moment in my life, I completely lost confidence in "the system" and the honesty of people in politics. Any mention of similar situations made me sick.

Then came the fall of 1943. It was a bit different from the others, I started at the Petit Seminaire (now The Collège de Montréal) to take my course in classics. It was our parish priest, Fr. Desjardins, convinced that I had a religious vocation and exceptional ability, who offered my parents a scholarship to defray my educational expenses. They had no other choice than to accept since they too thought that I wanted to become a priest. In fact at that time, I sincerely wanted to become a missionary. My piety and my exemplary moral rectitude were signs of this faith, but this fine project soon became another false start.

Accustomed in primary school to learning everything by heart, thanks to my exceptional memory, I soon became aware that at college this would not be sufficient to come in first! To begin with, the competition was very strong, and I realized that there were other students who were as intelligent as I was and, to make matters worse, some of them seemed even more brilliant than I was. I had a hard time swallowing this and took refuge in aggression and resentment while accusing my teachers of favoritism.

For me to come fourth or fifth out of forty-three students would be a shameful fall from grace! I continued to study, but with less motivation; I only ran on my memory and thus excelled in some subjects to the detriment of others in which analysis and judgment were important elements of learning. I still wanted to be a priest and a missionary in Africa, but none of my friends showed any interest in coming with me, even when I tried to sell the "adventure" side of this wonderful vocation. Since I could not see myself as an ordinary little parish priest or even a secular one, I imagined myself in the jungle among wild animals and primitive tribes...in the absence of adventure, I would immediately demand an important ministry in a large diocese as bishop or even cardinal. At least I would wear a biretta and sash of red!

But God doesn't love the proud, and he had my plans changed or rather those of the priest and my family. The arrival of puberty plunged me into deep confusion. At fifteen I knew the forbidden pleasure of sexual relations and masturbation as its replacement. Feelings of guilt overwhelmed me, and I was always in a state of mortal sin since I was too proud to confess such vile and abnormal acts....

However, despite all my remorse, I kept my faith and I thought that the God whom I loved would perhaps forgive me if I didn't start again. But rather than getting better, I lost control and went looking for more and more excitement. For me sexuality became a form of escape into a soft world of pleasure and eroticism. My religious vocation disappeared into a sensual vortex, and my attitude to life began to change radically. From then on I thought that happiness on earth was only possible on a material level and that stories of religious life were fairy tales.

I was terrified at the thought that I would soon have to tell my parents and the parish priest of Saint-Germain that I was not continuing on this path. I was sad and so sorry, unable to forgive myself for this defection that made me so sick at heart. In grade eleven (the year of my "Belles Lettres"), I took my courage in both hands and told the news to my parents. The priest tried to change my mind, but to no avail. My father warned me not to "waste" my classical education and to at least try to become a doctor or a lawyer. But I was completely disoriented, I had lost all sense of reality surrounding me. I was already gorging myself on thoughts of material wealth and eternal love.

Going into my last year of classical studies ("Rhetoric") or grade twelve, I was seventeen and my self-opinion was inflated at the thought of graduating. Since I was no longer first in class, I had to compensate with sports in order to satisfy my all-consuming vanity. I played centre in hockey and I wore number ten on my sweater. Needless to say I could never accept the loss of a face-off. If the opposing centre had the misfortune of stealing the puck from me, I would make him pay by the end of the game by spearing or crushing him on the boards! My growing pride began to show up more and more in all my actions, and I gradually became a violent and nasty person toward all those who dared challenge me.

In order to make myself still more dominating, I took up boxing and I trained solely to be able to hit harder. I went after the punching bag with my bare fists like a crazy man; my knuckles split and I would bleed from both hands. This rage welling up in me, this constant rebellion, which assaulted me, and those acts of aggression against others scared and saddened me, but I was powerless, I had lost control of my emotions, and I couldn't figure out what was happening to me.

My reputation as a troublemaker and the dirtiest player on the team followed me for years; quick as lightning, I always struck first and was nicknamed "Shivers." Opponents watched for me and warned each other to avoid that "damned little number ten" like the plague. Once again I had to be number one in every sport or activity. It was the same for tennis, baseball, skiing, or anything else that I undertook.

I felt like a time bomb that was about to explode at any moment; I couldn't take it anymore. My hostility began showing up at home in response to my father's orders that I could no longer accept. Something was bound to happen because I was about to crack under the pressure, and I couldn't think straight anymore.... Then, for the first time, the question came to me; why not end it all and finish this life that never gives me more than a second or third place? Wouldn't this be the stroke of brilliance that would at least put me first in people's conversations?

What a false start to life!

2

Destined for Failure

At the age of seventeen, I was very active in sports. They had become my favorite escape and a place of power where I could continue to dominate others, so I thought...So, after the game, most of the guys showed up at the "Chapel," what we called our local tavern,* in order to cool off and have a beer or two. Once again I set myself apart by being proud of the fact that I didn't drink that "vile" alcohol; no, the champion only drinks soda pop!

It was then that one of my buddies shot at me: "Hey, André, the reason why you don't drink is because you're afraid of your father!"

It didn't take much to get to me and my easily wounded pride.

"Me, afraid of my father? You must be kidding! I'll show you who's afraid of whom!"

Without knowing it, my buddy, by provoking me in this way, gave me the opportunity to do something that would be a lifesaver at the time....I discovered THE way to escape, to numb my hurt and remorse, and to give myself the illusion that a successful life was still possible and doable. This way of escaping, the alcohol I drink, brings me peace, an immense feeling of well-being and an end to my distress, my fears and sense of guilt.

Yes, alcohol makes me perfect in my own eyes and, when drunk at last, I sink into the most stupendous

*A drinking establishment for men only

13

dreams, I become a near demigod impervious to any weakness. I have finally found a faithful friend in the alcohol that becomes THE answer to all my problems. I can now confront the world that makes me so afraid, and I become a higher being who can forever satisfy every whim of its overbearing vanity. I am unaware, (or, unconsciously, I don't want to know) that my drinking is abnormal. The reality is, that I can never stop drinking before I am completely drunk. This behavior soon causes me a lot of problems and totally changes who I am. I become hostile toward my father who tries to cure me of my "weakness" and thus restricts my freedom.

Some of the other students at the college had had enough of my abuse and went looking for revenge. One day one of them put a couple of *Life* magazines in my locker and then told the discipline prefect that I had "forbidden" reading material. The prefect, or "SS" as he was called, opened my locker, found the offending magazines, which were on the "Index"* and reported me to the college superior, who summoned me to his office. My father was also asked to come to the meeting. When he arrived, the superior told us that I was now expelled. With graduation and final exams only two months away, I was barred from college! I now had to pass my exams "ex collegio" at l'Université de Montréal, which had deigned to accept me at a special exam sitting in June.

Motivated by vengeance and wounded pride, I passed my exams "Magna Cum Laude."** The university published my results and, to my great surprise, my father and I were again invited to meet with the college superior. Then and there he made the unheard-of suggestion that I transfer my exam results from the University to the Collège de Montréal. Unbelievable! After having expelled me, he now wanted to raise the overall college

*A list of publications restricted by the Roman Catholic Church
**With great distinction

14

average by stealing my grades!

Everything had definitely been done to get me to rebel. I made it very clear that I refused the "favor" that the college had offered me, as I slammed the door behind me. But I still felt ridiculed and unjustly treated. My father could not stop me from swearing. I worked myself into an uncontrollable rage and we almost came to blows. But alcohol came to my rescue, and I decided to drown all my feelings with a two-day bender. I came to, full of remorse and with waves of fear washing over me. I decided that enough was enough. I could never go home because I was too ashamed and too angry with the whole world. I felt beaten by despair and totally abandoned.

In the spring of 1950, I rented a room on Lorne Crescent Street for a week. It was close to downtown, and I was friends with the janitor who was an ex-con. He drank with me, and when he saw how messed up I was, he tried to encourage me by saying that he could find me a job. But I wanted no part of that. I was determined to end my flawed and unfair life once and for all.

We were sitting in the Pine Avenue Tavern when he began to raise his voice while saying that I was only a spoiled kid complaining about nothing. It didn't take any more than that for me to start punching him out. I no longer recognized myself. I acknowledged with fear the violence that lived within me. I returned to lock myself in my room. I looked back at the years of my short life and convinced myself that I should stop hurting my mother, betraying my father, putting down my friends, and continuing my downward slide. I did not have the courage to keep going, and I opened the gas valves on the stove. This odorless natural gas would soon carry me to a far better world.

But this was not to be, this was not my fate. . . . There was a violent explosion followed by a flash fire. The janitor, who had escaped the flames, told the fire fighters that I was still inside, and they came and saved me from the blaze. I was still only half-conscious when they questioned me about it, and I remembered almost nothing of what had happened. But I can still hear the janitor telling the police that he had caused the explosion when he had forgotten to turn off the gas after he had cooked his meal. Why did this man, whom I had just beaten up, protect me? I have no other explanation than this: he was guided by the hand of God. Totally shaken by these events, and humiliated by my failure to commit suicide, I hid everything from my parents and asked them to give me another chance and allow me to go back home.

I was now nineteen years old and my alcohol consumption continued growing rapidly, to the great despair of my father, who harassed me continually. My mother tried to protect me as well as she could. But I saw the deep worry in her eyes that came from watching me gradually destroy my chances for success in life despite all the talents that I had started out with.

Her turmoil caused me much pain, and I felt guilty when faced with her suffering. I wanted so much to change the way I behaved, but alcohol and pride were too strong and I continued to sink into hopelessness.

After finishing my second year in Philosophy at the Université de Montréal, I had to quickly choose a career. My father was not happy when I decided to enroll in the School of Industrial Relations at the same university. He accused me of being a communist, a socialist, a rabble-rouser, and a failure. How was it that his wonderful André, so intelligent and talented, would shame his family by going into Social Science? His reaction and this great disappointment on my family's part were quite understandable given the times we lived in. It was the Duplessis*era when company-union relations were at their lowest.

*Maurice Duplessis premier of Québec 1936-1939, 1944-1959. His government was characterized as pro-business, pro-Catholic, anti-communist, anti-socialist, and anti-union.

I made this choice simply because, as far as I was concerned, it was the shortest route to a master's degree. Firmly believing that happiness was to be found in a world of money and material wealth, I took the quickest road to get there. When I had definitely decided to go into Industrial Relations, my father forced me to pay for all my educational expenses. I found student summer jobs, worked weekends to make ends meet, and despite everything, I managed to go on drinking more and more. At twenty-one, I already had the "eye-opener" syndrome. In order to function I had to have a drink before going to my first class. I had an alcohol dependency, and I turned in on myself more and more. I was on the dizzying slope leading to my inevitable loss.

With my B.A. in hand, I quit my summer job three weeks after I started, so I could go to celebrate my success with friends. It was a Friday night in June when I left for Ile Perrot, and I didn't stop bingeing until I returned to university in September. Staying drunk for weeks on end gave me a split personality in which I became the other André, a dangerous and unpredictable alcoholic, an irrational being lost in the horrors of alcohol.

Little by little I underwent a metamorphosis into the characters of Doctor Jekyll and Mr. Hyde. That summer I became friends with Gilles, who drank a lot, was as arrogant as I was, and who thought he was above everyone else. We rapidly became the scourge of all the bars and hotels between Sainte-Anne de Bellevue and Ile Perrot. We were the troublemakers and the instigators of fights and brawls in every local tavern. Gilles was a waiter at one of the hotels and always had enough change in his pockets to keep buying me drinks. I already knew how to sleep outdoors and to take advantage of empty summer cottages. My training as a vagrant had begun.

We both had great opinions of ourselves. We were the best fighters and the finest dancers, the smartest and the most "in." We pretended to be the best lovers in the place. We were always about to seduce the most girls possible.

What a life! It was so great to really believe that we were better than anyone else around.

My bloated ego had never had it so good.

But when morning came I awoke from these false dreams and illusions to find myself overcome by panic and the shakes. Guilt and remorse birthed this other André, a hypersensitive person, utterly incapable of controlling the least of his emotions. I always had to rush to find the drink that would rebury that horrible feeling of weakness and get me back on my mirage merry-go-round.

Autumn came. I had to go back home. My parents believed that I had been working out of town all summer. They had no idea that I was lounging around nearly all of the time with nothing else to do but drink and fight. Life's routine began again, and I felt a bit more secure within my family, except that there was a price to pay: I had a curfew, and I couldn't cut classes. I had a very hard time accepting these limits, and the poisoned relations with my father picked up where they had left off.

In 1953, my final year of university, I pursued my studies while shackled to the major handicap of my alcoholism. I was in an intern program for two days a week at the Québec Ministry of Labor's Conciliation and Arbitrating Services Department. Jacques was my program supervisor. He was one of the conciliators for the Honorable Antonio Barette, the Minister of Labor for the Province of Québec. Remember Jacques because he will show up in another chapter of this book.

The internship went well, and Jacques and I became friends and bridge partners. I was an excellent player because bridge is a game of memory, and memory was definitely my strong suit. It was just about my only ability that was not yet affected by alcohol. The year came to an end. I did very well on my exams and on my master's thesis. It was solely through the strength of my pride and my exceptional memory that I accomplished this tour de force. I didn't deserve it, and I didn't seriously learn anything because everything began and ended with a drink. And, now that I knew everything, because I had a university degree, the world of work was mine, as were the ignoramuses of the business world!

My problem with alcohol worsened and followed me in the workplace. None of my bosses knew the job to be done better than I did, and I tolerated no authority. I was often absent, mostly on the Fridays when I got paid and Monday mornings when I shook so much that I had to drink until noon to be in good enough shape to show up at work.

The reason I was able to keep my job was due to that of my father's influence in the business world and the good relations he had with my superiors. My bosses always told him the same thing: "Georges, your son is really talented, but whenever he takes a drink, he is totally useless. It's really too bad!"

Forced by my father's threats and insistence, I made promise after promise to take control of my drinking. Painfully, and with great difficulty, I managed to quit for a few weeks. But I was soon off again when I sold myself on the idea that my problem was not the alcohol, but a lack of understanding on the part of my bosses, my father, and my coworkers, in short, the whole world.

My irresponsibility did not take long to manifest itself: within a three-year period, I quit working at Northern Electric three times. They rehired me four times in various positions without ever succeeding in satisfying my requirements. The last time I quit just before they were about to fire me because of my repeated absences and chronic insubordination.

During the winter I took up downhill skiing. With very little money, I had to be satisfied with the hills on Mount Royal where the student ski tow pass was only fifty cents a day. But at the university, there were rich little daddys' girls, and one of them offered to pay for me if I would accompany her to Saint Sauveur for a weekend in the Laurentians. What luck!

From that time on, I stayed at the Hotel Nadeau every weekend. We would board the "Petit train du Nord," with anywhere from ten to fifteen revellers in our group. On Sunday afternoon tradition dictated that the Hotel Nadeau gang had to take on the Nymark Hotel gang. For no apparent reason, the fighting would break out. The "French Canadians" fought against the Irish, and the hotel would empty. Then everyone would calm down again, and except for a few bruises, no one was ever seriously hurt. Then the Anglos and Francos would reestablish friendly relations and resume celebrating and dancing together. For my part, I had to go aside to drink more than the others in order to relax, to avoid beginning another brawl. Once again, I thought I was tougher than all those weaklings.

As far as my love life was concerned, I was unable to maintain any lasting relationships; no woman was good enough to meet my physical and emotional needs. I was always on the lookout for the most beautiful girl in order to impress my friends and family. I succeeded in finding rare beauties. I used to show them off to draw envious stares from those around me. I don't have to add that these relationships had nothing to do with love, and that the emptiness created by my selfishness weighed heavily upon me. I wondered what was happening to me. I was unable to recognize my problem and was powerless before the uncontrollable thirst that was consuming my very being. I still firmly believed that happiness came from money, power, prestige, and material possessions. I was in a constant search for these seemingly essential means of satisfying my ambition. Actually I was looking for love and friendship, and I deceived myself by thinking I could buy them.

Thanks to my father (once again), I landed an important

position as a manager in an American electronics company. It didn't take me long to find out that the company president had a serious drinking problem. I soon became friends with him. In less than six months, he gave me a promotion and doubled my salary and expense account. Now I could drink as much as I wanted, buy a big car, a yacht, and any other little thing that would amaze and deceive my onlooking admirers. In spite of the alcohol abuse, the all-nighters, and the escapades, I was quite successful in my work thanks to my still-functioning memory. I decided to write a procedures manual for transport management and Customs and Excise laws and regulations. I already considered myself an expert on the subject, and I sent my manual to the federal government in Ottawa to have the content approved before publishing it.

At the time my father was the chief appraiser for the Port of Montréal and was also the head of the Customs and Excise Canada office. The federal government had long considered him an expert. Imagine his surprise when he received a copy of my government-approved manual! His colleagues in Ottawa and Montréal congratulated him on having such a brilliant son who was following in his father's footsteps. However, I had never let my father know about my project, and he was very upset and disappointed that I hadn't consulted him from the beginning. Me, consult my father? You have got to be kidding! I was already much better than he was, and I had proved it. I was so self-satisfied! But the alcohol slyly continued its work, and I became more and more irresponsible. I no longer produced the normal results expected of me. I felt that I was gradually losing all control of my life, and I was often overcome by dark thoughts, usually when I drank alone.

I haunted the upscale bars and clubs of west Montréal where, always dissatisfied with who I was, I invented personas and assumed different characters to indulge my vanity. For example, I became a gynecologist in the Piccadilly

Room of the Hotel Mount Royal, a test pilot at Café Tourbillon, a Korean war hero, and a U.S. Air Force captain working for the United Nations, etc. So that was the beginning of my personality splits, living lies and totally weird ideas. My life would soon tilt dangerously toward the abyss of incoherence punctuated by more and more frequent blackouts. But this pride cost me dearly, and I ran up debts at a frightening speed. I was gradually excluded from the bars and hotels in the west end of the city, and I had to go to drink in lower-class establishments, which were, more often than not, the taverns and clubs in Montréal's east end.

During the summer, I went to my parents' cottage at Saint-Placide where I had my yacht and my credit was still good at the local hotel. I met several girls whom I could drink and dance with. I never met my true love, but I found physical contact and great sexual gymnastics. Finally I realized that instead of finding happiness in money and possessions, I felt loneliness and emptiness all around me. Alcohol made me a different person, "the other André," the one who was violent, lying, dishonest, and totally irresponsible. How could I regain my temporary balance and my reason when I was inhabited by this obsession? I could see hell approaching, and I was powerless to stop it. I was in the depths of despair, I had lost my self-confidence and I had no faith or hope. My teetering soul was in total panic.

Then one fine day in the summer of 1957, on a weekend at my parents' cottage, an event happened that would alter my whole life. As I look toward the beach, I see two girls getting out of my brother's and his friend's boat. One of them immediately catches my attention. I am overcome with a feeling that I have never felt before, and in my deepest self, I know that she is the one whom I have been always waiting for.

That day my excitement grew, and my soul was no longer alone. It had found its twin, its other half, that it would never again have to look for. Would that wonderful encounter with Claudette be enough to lift my spirits and to stop me from continuing to destroy all aspects of my life? Would this first true love give me the hope and the motivation to resolve my alcohol problem and stop my dizzying slide into the abyss, to the rock bottom of my sickness?

It would take a poor understanding of the power of alcohol to be able to answer yes to these questions, because nothing up to now could block the path leading to my self-destruction. Not doctors, not psychiatrists, not other therapists, not even my mother's love could uproot this uncontrollable thirst and this terrible craving to get drunk more and more often.

This new love, strong as it was, would also end up smashing into the unavoidable wall of my powerlessness to assume my responsibilities, to take control of my emotions and my hypersensitivity. What a dilemma! I now had everything that I needed to succeed in life: I had an important and well-paying job. I still had my health, and my reputation was not yet beyond saving. And...I had this marvelous love that had just arrived like a gift from heaven. Any man who was the least bit normal, would take his courage in both hands and put some order back into his life. But the sick person that I had become, was powerless to change his life. I had lost the freedom of choice. Although seemingly in control of my consumption whenever I was with Claudette, I went straight to my drunken hell the moment I left her.

After our outings, I would drive her back to her place in Lachute, but on the way back to Montréal, I would stop at the first bar that I saw and start on another drunk. I was relatively sober only when I was with Claudette because I knew for certain that if she discovered my secret life as an inveterate drinker, she would leave in a flash. I felt caught in a dead end. On the one hand, I had a true love that consumed me, and on the other hand, I had this damned alcohol that controlled my life. I knew that sooner or later, if I continued on this road, I would destroy this happiness in spite of everything. Whenever I thought of this, panic would overcome me. In desperation I decided to put myself in a situation in which I would have to stop drinking. I thought I had the answer. If I became engaged to Claudette, I would surely have the courage to change my life in order to save our love and our eventual marriage!

I kept telling her how I loved her and repeated this phrase: "I adore you next to God, and I will love you forever." I was completely sincere at the time, and I was convinced that that was going to save our love, this love so wonderfully spiritual and so profoundly tender. Yes, I would love her forever. Yes, I would conquer this alcohol demon!

During the Christmas holidays of 1957–58, I gave Claudette an engagement ring, and I sincerely believed that my problem was solved. I had no choice, so I would drink no more! I abstained for several days, and I thought that I had succeeded in mastering my drinking habit, not knowing that my first glass would trigger an unquenchable thirst. I was certain that I could stop after a few refills. I now know that this effort was doomed to failure in spite of all my good intentions.

I resumed drinking in a big way, and there was no more stopping my thirst. I went on a ten-day bender and was overcome by remorse. The whole situation was hopeless, and I intuited that I would lose the love of my life if she ever discovered me in such a woeful condition. I didn't have the courage to get in touch with her and I disappeared. A new escapade into alcohol helped me to forget this failure and to drown my deep distress. What a betrayal for her. What a monster I had thus become by destroying such a beautiful dream.

All this time I was absent from work, with business trips and important meetings as my excuse. I only went to the office to pick up my paycheck and to submit my expense account. My bosses were very aware of my abnormal behavior and my diminished productivity. At the beginning of March they asked me to a business lunch. I agreed to meet with them and prepared my defense, knowing full well that the reason for the meeting was not to congratulate me. The company president and the comptroller awaited me at Ruby Foo's at noon. I met them with an air of calm and confidence.

"André," they said to me, "your results up until a few months ago have been excellent, but we have now come to warn you that your problem with alcohol could threaten your career with the company. If you don't stop your abusive drinking, you risk being fired!"

It didn't take more than that to cut me to the quick! How could they accuse me of drinking too much when the president himself was often so drunk that he needed me to help him make it home? No, it shouldn't be said by these stuffed shirts that I drank too much! it was necessary to save face and provide a justification for my behavior because yes, there would always be an explanation for my wild and irresponsible actions. I had one ready made.

So I explained to my American colleagues that if I was celebrating more often than I should, it was because I was making the most of my last days as a bachelor. And I went on to say: "You don't have to do a thing. Soon all that will stop because, two weeks from now, I'm getting engaged and in three weeks I'll be married! After that the party will be over and I'll be a model employee from now on."

This is another example of a desperate situation in which the alcoholic becomes entangled when, like a rat, he is caught in a corner. And with that I saved my pride and kept my job. But I was far from thinking that everything would work out and that my bald-faced lie would become reality. Pleased with my "solution," my bosses bought me a double Scotch, wished me happiness and many children and left, their problem solved.

Alone at the bar, I stirred the ice in my glass and really asked myself whom I could get engaged to in two weeks and whom I would marry in three. I had no idea, and I realized that in saving my pride, I had become a galley slave on a sinking ship. I loved Claudette too much to make her share my life of misery. Besides, I hadn't talked with her for almost two months. She had gotten in touch with my mother to try and find me, but she too had no idea where I was. For weeks I had been going from one motel to the next. I was in full flight as a prelude to my coming vagrancy.

But destiny is often unknowable and full of almost unbelievable surprises. So now, on the same day that I gave my word to my bosses that I would be getting married in three weeks, life arranged for my crazy scheme to actually work! Contrary to all expectations and against all odds, I really would get married in three weeks. Coincidence or destiny?

I was a bit tipsy when I came out of Ruby Foo's. I jumped into my Cadillac Eldorado and drove to my friend Claude's service station to get some gas. This was where I usually went because he was a long-time buddy and above all because he always offered me a drink every time we met. It was the only place that I went to on a regular basis where my mother could call me to beg me to come back home. That very afternoon Claude informed me that Monique had left a message and wanted me to call her back as soon as possible. Monique was a beautiful young girl among so many others whom I briefly went out with during the summer at Saint-Placide. She was a girl whose physical attributes and fiery temperament had attracted me, and no one liked to take a drink more than she did. Our relationship had only been a temporary one and had tended to be more erotic than loving. What then did she want from me?

My father continued to harass me (with good reason) to

make me stop drinking. I had only one thing on my mind, and that was to find a way or a good excuse to leave home as quickly as possible for once and for all. I would soon be presented with a solution. I had the brilliant idea of using Monique to help me escape from my father's influence. I called her.

"Hello, Monique, it's so nice to hear from you."

We engaged in small talk, and I gave her the impression that I was still really interested in her and that presently I had no other woman in my life.

What a lie, what a fraud! My clouded spirit tried to make the haunting image of Claudette disappear. Hadn't I just become secretly engaged to her a few weeks ago? At this point my emotions and my sensitivity were put to sleep by alcohol and I lost my ability to think. While torn by remorse, I succeeded in momentarily chasing any thought of my only real love from my mind. It had become unattainable. And so I choked my love to death by my inability to overcome the cause of my woes. My powerlessness to heal a sickness that I didn't know I had and that killed my soul as well.

And Monique asked me: "Would you like to be my date for my birthday party on March the 9th?"

My mind acted quick as lightning and decided to risk everything: "Yes, Monique, I would be very happy to, on one condition: that we become engaged on March 15th and we get married on March 22nd."

I said all this more than a bit hypocritically and with a sense of humor. It took some time to sink in. Seeing her hesitation, I forced it home by saying as seriously as I could that if she refused, I wouldn't accept her invitation.

As unbelievable as it seems, Monique said yes to everything. On the same day as I had promised my bosses that I would get married in three weeks, I had succeeded in this outrageous masquerade! And now I had solved all my problems. I was going to get rid of my father by leaving home in less than a month. I had saved my job, and I also realized that I was about to marry a girl who enjoyed tossing down a drink as much as I did. Her father was a doctor, so she was rich. At the same time, I had solved my problem with Claudette before she ever found out why I had to run away. I would later realize that it was my unconscious fear of forever destroying this great love that made me act like this without knowing if some day she could ever forgive this despicable act of betrayal.

I gave the news to my mother, who tried everything to dissuade me from this insane course of action. She was unsuccessful. I asked her if I could come home soon to get ready for my wedding. My father was furious, but he finally agreed to let me back in the house, being of the opinion that the marriage would perhaps straighten me out and that I would stop drinking and finally become a "responsible" adult.

During the call, my mother told me that Claudette had repeatedly tried to get in touch with me and was wondering what had happened to me. Because of my condition, my mother hadn't given her my friend Claude's number, knowing full well that she would end up finding out what terrible shape her son was in. As for my mother and Claudette, the two people whom I loved most dearly, I could barely imagine the hell that I had put them through, especially my former fiancée.

Eaten by remorse, driven crazy by the situation I had created and terrified by the idea of telling Claudette the news, I again took refuge in my bottled illusions. Fortified by the false courage of more alcohol, and now sufficiently anesthetized, I decided to call her at work.

"You want to know what has happened to me? You want my news? Well, I'll tell you. I'm becoming engaged in two weeks, and I'm getting married on March 22nd. That's it."

There was total silence at the other end of the line. It

was a terrible shock for this innocent victim of my sense-lessness. She didn't know what to say, and anyway I didn't give her the time or the opportunity to respond. I hung up right away. I thought that if I acted brutally enough with Claudette, she would forget me more easily and thank God for being saved from such a maniac. How heartless! My nastiness would only have hurt her more deeply. What a screw up!

After the call, I drank until I passed out, trying in vain to drown my grief and to erase this nightmare that haunted me. I knew that I had committed an irreparable error and that the only thing remaining for me to do was to destroy the other parts of my life. I left the motel and went back home to my parents' place with death in my soul.

In my obstinacy, and pushed by my cocksure pride, I nervously prepared for the coming weeks, and I made sure that Monique's parents were supporting me: her father convinced the priest to cancel the publication of the banns so that the marriage could take place on March 22nd. With only ten days to go, I decided to have some teeth extracted and had a dental plate in place forty-eight hours later. There was nothing better to take away the pain than a good drinking spree. I was off again. I disappeared for three days, and everyone was worried that I might not make it back in time for the wedding.

As I was out of cash, I thought I should go home and get myself dolled up for the celebration. We would be honey-mooning at Daytona Beach in Florida at a motel that Monique's father had recommended. Besides, he was paying for everything. He even lent me his credit card! I had really hit the jackpot and we, Monique and I, could drink ourselves silly. The company gave me a three-week vacation and a television set for a wedding present. I had duped them too. It was a real pleasure to put one over on those smart Americans, who had fallen for my smoke and mirrors. But it was complete arrogance on my part to believe that I was out of danger just because I was the protégé of the president of the company.

After the ceremony, we finally left for Daytona Beach. We often had to stop for gas. We had to stop more often to get "gassed" ourselves. There were two of us drinking now. When we got there, we bought some food and more alcohol. We consummated our marriage, which would soon become as indigestible as our drinking. The quarrels had already begun and our relationship soured. Monique scolded me for drinking too much beer and not enough of the "high class beverages." I retorted that she drank too much vodka and that she didn't even know how to boil an egg. It was already obvious that after being married for only a week, the basis for our relationship was fragile at the very least. How long could this partnership survive without any real love? The reason for our marriage was not to make a life together, but a pretext for the two of us to escape parental authority, to be "free," to be able to drink without any restrictions.

During these two weeks of the trip, the image of Claudette, the only woman whom I ever loved, kept returning to my mind, and I was sadder than ever. Right in the middle of my honeymoon, I decided to write her to tell her that I had made a mistake and that it really ought to be she who should be there with me in Daytona. It hurt me to think of the suffering that I would cause her by writing to her. I felt like an executioner, a torturer who couldn't escape this infernal circle. The memory of Claudette haunted me from then on, and I could never again forget her features. Perhaps this breakup was meant to happen to make me realize how much I loved her and what price my alcoholism was going to make me pay for these irresponsible acts of mine.

When we returned we stayed with Monique's parents for a month. We didn't have enough money to buy furniture, let alone a house. I decided to rent an old furnished summer cottage by the lake at Saint-Placide to give us time to find a place to stay before fall came. One would have to be totally unconscious and full of booze to live in a dump like that. Think of it, I was a director of a large company, I owned a Cadillac Eldorado, Monique had her Austin Healy, and both of them were parked outside this rundown cottage. We drank, we danced, we drank some more, and we laughed...then we cried. We knew that, despite Monique's pregnancy, we were at a dead end, in a whirlpool that inexorably led to divorce sooner or later.

I dared to invite my first fiancée, Claudette, to a party that I was throwing at my cottage. To my great surprise, she showed up with friends. I was awestruck. When I saw her again, she was so beautiful and more ravishing than ever. I was rocked to the core of my very being. I kept everything inside me, and I pretended to be happy by adopting a carefree, easy style. Seeing Claudette again plunged me into a sadness that I had a hard time covering up, but pride and alcohol were stronger than everything else, and I knew that I could hide behind them to calm my agitation a bit and stifle the pain that ate away at my soul. I had often told her: "Claudette, I adore you next to God, and I will love you forever." That's the truth! I could never again escape from that love that I had so cruelly and stupidly destroyed.

Things got extremely out of hand, summer was over, and the debts accumulated. I was spending at least twice as much as I was earning, and my vanity cost me dearly. I was celebrating big time. I wanted to buy love and friendship by impressing everyone. I dropped a bundle on a wild party that I held at the cottage. Full orchestra with singers, open bar with uniformed waiters, hot and cold buffet, fireworks, yacht rides and water skiing, loudspeakers in the trees, important guests, there was everything. Nothing was finer or more expensive, come and admire me, come and love me, come and see the number one guy in Saint-Placide!

And then fall came. There was a brutal return to the reality of accounts to settle and bills to pay. Up to my ears in debt, I didn't even have the means to buy furniture and rent an apartment. I was reduced to living with my in-laws, who were generous enough to welcome me along with their daughter. It was a humiliating situation when one came to realize that the main reason we got married was for each of us to be able to leave home. What an attack on my self-esteem to have to beg like that for my bread.

I was unable to meet my obligations and to respect the financial agreements that I had undertaken. To try to get my hands on more money, I inflated my expense account and I sold things that I had taken from the company. The short of it was that I had become an embezzler and a petty thief. But this extra money didn't even go to paying off my debts or covering my NSF checks. Instead of solving my problems, I had created another by drinking more and by feeling guiltier than ever. My thirst for alcohol and escape ruled everything and I became a slave to my obsession.

In September of 1958, the president of the company died. He had also been my drinking buddy and my job protector. Not long after his death, his replacement (a really sober guy!) and the company comptroller got together and called me to his office to finally give me the bad news. Not only had my marriage not solved my alcohol problem (it had done exactly the opposite), they had also discovered the fraud that I had committed, so they thanked me for my services. As the prince of a man he was, in exchange for my unconditional resignation, he agreed to not press charges for theft and embezzlement. The only choice I had was to accept his offer, and so I resigned immediately.

The fine material world that I had created around my little self came crashing down. At the same time, I saw my great dreams of opulence and freedom fly away. Good-bye to my golden calf of pride, farewell to my sacred cow of not caring, bye-bye to the pork barrel of my arrogance, so long to my golden goose of extravagance. Adieu, calf, cow, pig, and goose. So now, I had been presented with another reason for drinking. Because my employer had fired me and had not understood that despite my "moderate" consumption of alcohol, and a few occasional slip-ups, I was still their best employee. I felt attacked, judged, and condemned without just cause and moreover, I was greatly misunderstood and the victim of my superiors' incompetence.

Poor me! I have every reason to be sorry about the way I am. God, am I ever thirsty!

Neither my father-in-law nor anyone else wanted to help me out financially, and I saw myself being forced into personal bankruptcy. So I put everything I had left into receivership: the keys to my shiny Cadillac and more than eighteen thousand dollars in debts. For the proud one I was, this episode in my life was so very painful and set off my dizzying slide into the hell of my sickness, an inexorable descent to rock bottom that humans rarely reach.

Without realizing it, due to being blinded by shame and rendered unconscious by my daily drinking, I was approaching a progressive state of madness, which reduced me to a spiritual and moral nothing and made my soul plunge into an abyss of despair. Other distressing news, Monique was pregnant and I couldn't see how I would ever be able to support her and take care of a newborn child. It would take a miracle for me to get out of the hole that I was stuck in. Neither my bankruptcy nor the Lacombe Act* would help my financial recovery. To add to that, my reputation had taken a blow, and it was nearly impossible to find a decent job.

After being unemployed for a few weeks , I turned up in a job at Pascal Hardware as a manager-salesman in the sports section. I barely made sixty dollars a week. That much could neither satisfy my needs nor pay off my debts. I began to wonder of what use were all those diplomas lying around in the bottom of a drawer somewhere, and how was

*The Québec bankruptcy protection act

it possible for me to be in this situation? I was incapable of admitting that my alcohol problem was the only real cause. I persisted in finding excuses and in getting really drunk, blaming each and every one for my suffering. To satisfy my excesses, I was forced to be dishonest, so once again I found the means to defraud my employer and thus add even more weight to my feelings of guilt and remorse.

After work I had to take the Provincial Transport Company bus from the east terminal to go home (actually to my father-in-law's place on the south shore). Fortunately, there was a bar quite close to the terminal, and I regularly went there to pass the time before the bus left. Since the bus was on an hourly schedule, I had lots of time to get drunk and because I was unable to control my thirst, I had to jump on the last bus at 11:00 P.M. I don't know how many times I fell asleep, only to wake up at the end of the line in Granby, fifty miles from home.

Totally shamefaced, I had to call my father-in-law to come and get me because the buses had stopped running and I had no money to pay for a taxi. As a doctor, my father-in-law quickly saw that I suffered from a serious problem and that his daughter had found herself an ideal drinking partner. He let me know that it concerned him, and he asked me to moderate my drinking. But nothing gave. My state worsened and I became more and more arrogant. Violence and aggression gained more momentum and venomous hate, the poison of resentment, permeated my soul.

I would no longer put up with this mediocre life. I was sick of my powerlessness, and the psychosis growing in my mind had made me dangerous.

It was now November 1959, and things were out of control. Monique lost her baby, her father had decided that he would do the delivery himself at home, and he could not have foreseen the complications of a breech birth. I lost a son! What a good excuse to again drown another sorrow and to leave once more in search of oblivion. When I returned from a three-day drunk, I told my in-laws that I could no longer live under the same roof with them and that I had decided to rent an apartment and take Monique with me, to have a normal life and perhaps even stop drinking. It was the first time that I admitted to having a problem with alcohol, but the reason was simple. I only said this to make it easier to leave and to get some sympathy from Monique's parents.

I moved into a tiny furnished apartment that I was able to rent by the month without a long-term lease. Monique moved in with me two days later and announced that she would try to stop drinking and make a new start. If she wanted to stop drinking and if she succeeded, I would lose my real reason for being with her, which was to have her as a drinking partner. I said that as far as I was concerned, it was not the fact of drinking that was my problem, but all the unforeseen circumstances that had hit me and all the people who didn't understand me.

Monique had now abstained for a week, and I was condemned to drink alone. Deep inside I knew that there was no way out and that my refusal to change would be my downfall. I went away for three days, and Monique threatened to leave me if I took off again. She had only been in the apartment for three weeks, and I had left her on her own.

On Christmas Eve 1959, her father came to get her, and to take a bit of revenge, he dumped out all the garbage cans in the apartment. I never saw Monique again. My wife had left, poor me, I had another reason to drink!

3

The Point of No Return

Free at last! Liberated from all responsibility and out from under my debts, thanks to my personal bankruptcy, I returned to fighting form and was ready to do anything in order to accomplish my material ambitions and my impractical fantasies. But bad luck kept hounding me. I lost my job because I was absent too often and was rude to the customers. In dire straits, I decided to ask my parents to let me move back home and to give me one last chance to find a job. My mother succeeded in convincing my father to take me back, but he insisted that I promise not to drink. Because I had no choice, I said yes for the umpteenth time and returned to the family bosom.

This temporary abstinence appeared to bring me luck. At the beginning of January (1960), I was hired by the National Employment Office of the federal government as an employment officer. My work place was at 10 Notre Dame Street East, at the corner of Saint Laurent Boulevard at the center of the popular downtown hotel and bar scene of the time. Since I wanted to stay with my parents for a few months to save up a bit of money, I didn't succumb to the temptation of visiting the clubs after work. I dutifully returned home under the watchful eye of my father, who checked my breath as he kept saying to my mother that I wouldn't be able to keep this up much longer. "Once a drunk, always a drunk" was one of his favorite sayings, and I well knew in my heart of hearts that he was right to doubt my ability to stay sober.

After a few months, I had become the best officer in the department. I was able to place twice as many unemployed people as the group average. My ever-present pride was useful enough. I still had my eye on first place. The head of my department called me to his office to find out why my technique was so effective and how I had managed to have such an almost unbelievable rate of success.

I felt my vanity going up a notch or two, I swelled with pride, I was full of self-admiration, and I deigned to say in my most haughty tone: "As you may be aware, sir, your officers haven't had the necessary training that would allow them to get the same results as I have. Perhaps you may not know it, but I have an M.A. in Industrial Relations, and I believe that it would be advantageous for my colleagues to have me give a few courses in worker endowments and other related subjects in order to deepen their understanding and to help them get better results."

"Splendid, André, what a good idea!"

So I embarked once again as a galley slave on the ship of fame, satisfied at last that my coworkers would appreciate my superior talents, that I could lord it over them by showing off my supposed expertise during the training sessions that they had allowed me to give. Some grumbled at the idea of coming in an hour early to attend a session given by erudite André. It has to be said that I had never in my life taught anyone. To feed my superiority complex, I took on a project that was beyond me and that rather scared me. Me, teach courses? What was I doing!

Why do I always try to dominate those around me? Of course it is to feed my insatiable ego, my morbid and unhealthy hunger for power.

But without alcohol for my fuel, I will never have enough confidence to stand up in front of a class of twenty adults, all older than I was, who would certainly try to trap me with trick questions. No, I couldn't do it, and, if I messed up and lost face, I probably wouldn't be able to get over it. So what to do? If I start drinking and my father finds out, he'll kick me out of the house. If I don't drink, I won't be able to give a single decent course. I'll be the laughing stock of the office, and I'll have to quit my job because I can't stand failure.

I didn't have the necessary humility to withdraw, I always had to recklessly forge ahead into the unknown in order to go even further into my delusion of superiority.

The only solution that offered me enough confidence to perform, was to take a drink first thing in the morning before the course. The effects of the alcohol would be gone by the time I had to go home after work. That way I could avoid my father's suspicions. Yet I knew full well that those few swallows in the morning would unleash a compulsive thirst for the rest of the day and it would be very hard to withstand for long the burning need to drink a bit more.

Thanks to my morning drink solution, I was able to give a course that seemed to satisfy my associates and even my superiors, to my great astonishment. But barely ten days had gone by before the morning drink was no longer enough. At lunchtime I went out to eat with my colleagues at the Hotel Saint Gabriel, renowned for its haute cuisine and wine cellar. The aperitifs and liqueurs were irresistibly attractive. My midday meal gradually expanded to three in the afternoon. I was dangerously close to an evening drink. I would soon come full circle and pass from a chronic illness to a hellish whirlpool of full-time alcoholism.

My father began to suspect that I had resumed drinking but my mother defended me while thinking that it was nothing but a temporary lapse caused by the stress of my new job and my unexpected responsibilities as a "teacher." For my part, I was still dissatisfied. I found my job lacking in scope and below my capacity. I was really full of myself! I looked for another challenge. I wanted to draw attention to my person and boost my reputation. And there it was, the chance I was waiting for: the position of President of the National Employees' Association of The Unemployment Insurance Commission (NEAUIC) was open for election.

I quickly announced my candidacy. I launched a lightning campaign and distanced myself from the other candidates with a program that was the most ambitious and interesting of all. I was elected by an overwhelming majority, and I received the applause and recognition that I was looking for. In less than four months on the job, I had become the lord of the office, the wise professor, and the national association president. But what had I taken to be able to do all of this? Nothing. The real question was more like: what was I drinking?

On a daily basis, my alcohol consumption was my number one concern, and the many association meetings at the Manoir des Oliviers were the excuse I gave to my father for coming home later and later. Of course, what was going to happen finally did happen. One fine evening in August, I totally lost control. I drank for three days straight and came to, utterly disoriented at Police Station number 10 on Saint Mathieu Street.

After getting in touch with my boss and fabricating a few lies to explain my absence, I arrived home to freshen up and change my clothes.

My father was lying in wait for me. He began shouting: "I knew it! You can't leave it alone, and you won't keep your word! You have no will, and I would be mistaken to trust you again; be assured that this is the last time I'll be taken in by you. So pack your bags and leave. Get out of here. Go and live with those useless friends of yours."

That night I rented a room downtown on Victoria Street, quite close to one of my favorite bars called "Le Café André." I went and cried in my beer and told my troubles to the barmaid, who pretended to understand me and sympathized with my lot. I got back to my tiny room around three in the morning. I felt very lonely and unhappy. I sensed that my whole world was falling apart around me ... I looked back on the last few years, and I was tortured with regret when I remembered all the stupid things I had done ... I could see Claudette, so beautiful in my imagination. I loved her so much, but it was impossible for me to get her back. Why, Lord? Why am I created like this? What a tragedy to destroy the finest things in my life. What a horrible sickness is this obsessive thirst, which makes me commit the worst acts of deception! No, I just don't understand. I felt my soul sliding into the wilderness of a future with no light. I went to sleep sobbing, with all of yesterday's beautiful dreams replaced by my worst nightmares.

With my absences from work increasing, and very dissatisfied with my situation, I quickly sought a promotion to polish my image. I sought new responsibilities because my present post could no longer sustain my deluded ambition. I applied for the position of regional director in competition with many others. Sure of my potential and my obvious ability, I already saw myself in the position since it seemed that all the other employees were far below me and had no chance of succeeding. What I had forgotten was that I only had a few months of seniority while others had been working for many years. The competition ended in October, and the post was awarded to the person with the most job seniority even if, in my opinion, he had neither my competence nor my breadth of experience? On top of that, he was one of my students.

Wounded in my false dignity, I asked for a top-level meeting to file my complaint to whomever and I threatened to resign if the promotion was not given to me. My immediate superior called me to his office and informed me that the selection committee would never reverse its decision and that I would be well advised to improve my work attendance if I wished to keep my present job. From my great height, I sharply retorted that a president of NEAUIC could not be treated like this and that anyway, I was giving him my resignation, knowing that I could no longer work with such a bunch of backward incompetents! I quit just like that, and found myself without a job.

Instead of working for the Unemployment Insurance Commission, I became a beneficiary all because of my arrogance and egotism. Consequently I would never learn to accept the smallest defeat. Would there ever come a day when I could resign myself to live on earth instead of constantly flying over the world in the clouds of my most presumptuous whims? I felt that I was increasingly losing control of my ability to reason and that new fears were emerging from my subconscious; so I quit my job in November of 1960 and was unemployed for the next five months.

Shortly before I left the National Placement Services Office, a young secretary named Jane invited me to room at her place with her mother and sister. Jane was carrying a torch for me and wanted to help me out. She introduced me to her mother and to her sister Beatrice. I was thus welcomed into the home of these three women. Those poor souls were very naive, and I took advantage of this by telling them the most incredible stories. Their gullibility encouraged me to make up new characters that transformed me at one time into a Korean war hero and another time into a test pilot for CF-100 and Voodoo jet aircraft. And why not into an RCMP (Royal Canadian Mounted Police) officer as well? I felt admired by these women. I received a great deal of satisfaction from them, and my vanity was well served. But I had to expand my circle of admirers, so I carried my characters with me to the clubs and bars that I went to. I was ready to do anything to draw attention to myself, to enhance my ego with a false pride all by satiating myself with my elixir of escape. Alcohol, forever alcohol.

During this period of almost six months of unemployment, my problem worsened and I felt that I was losing my self control, that my judgment was fading, and the rest of my abilities were noticeably weaker. Actually I was deeply troubled. I experienced panic and torment almost daily, and only an alcoholic stupor could bring me a time of peace in my tortured sleep. But waking revived the remorse, the guilt, and the obsession to drink again to forget more quickly. It was always the same merry-go-round that began at eight in the morning with the opening of the taverns. I sat down with others who were as sick as I was and planned my daily rounds.

My behavior deteriorated and I became more and more lost in the multiple personalities that I had invented for myself. It was the beginning of a crazy game that changed into a nightmare. I mostly drank in the clubs and taverns of west end Montréal where I was already known from better times when alcohol had not yet made me into someone else. Now I had become a man of violence, danger, lies, dishonesty, insolence, arrogance, and total unpredictability.

In the Piccadilly Room at the Hotel Mount Royal, I passed myself off as Dr. Andrew Wilson, a gynecologist. Most of the patrons seemed to believe me because of the many schemes that I used to trick them. I gave the bell boy two dollars to have me paged. "Dr. Wilson: Dr. Wilson, you're wanted on the telephone." I would stand up, smartly dressed, with my nose in the air and pretend to follow the bell boy to the phone so that everyone in the room could see me. When I returned to my table, I smiled at the women who had looked my way, and in no time at all, I got to know them. Then I would try to seduce them with my great medical knowledge. It was lots of fun until the day I met up with a woman doctor! At that point my pride took a hit, as I was unmasked, and to avoid the worst, I had to change hotels.

Always dissatisfied with my lot and my situation, I

continually changed my identity so I would be taken for someone else in order to satisfy my sick need to be seen as an important person. In one of my favorite clubs, the Cafe André, I became Captain André M. of the United States Air Force (USAF), and I was often sent on missions by the United Nations Security Council. To get my bar mates to swallow these totally fantastic stories, I rented a uniform, acquired false medals and forged papers, and sent myself fake telegrams to confirm my missions around the world.

One of these telegrams read: "Captain, your services are required for an inquest into the death of Dag Hammerskjöld, the U.N. Secretary General. Present yourself immediately at your base to arrange meetings with Moise Tschombe and Patrice Lumumba of The Congo. Signed, Capt. J. Clark, U.N. H.Q. New York."

What a lot of trouble to go to impress my gallery of onlookers, and all that without forgetting my part-time job as a test pilot at the Saint Hubert Air base. Indeed my madness progressed, and they were becoming somewhat wary. I was not short of indictable pranks, and one fine morning in March, I decided to buy all the properties situated on Dorchester Boulevard (now Boulevard Rene Levesque) between Peel and Guy Streets. I shared my intentions with my friends at the Crescent Tavern, who found it quite amusing that a guy on unemployment insurance would be fronting a transaction worth several million dollars.

Ignoring their sarcasm, I proceeded with my project and presented myself at the Dorchester Building Corporation to begin the negotiations. I passed myself off as a major real estate investor and asked the director to provide me with all the available leases for these properties. Believe it or not, he took me seriously and turned over two portfolios full of these treasured leases! When I returned to the tavern that afternoon, the guys couldn't believe their eyes and asked me where I was going to find the money to finance all that. Since I foresaw that the value of these properties would undergo a fivefold increase in the next ten years, I shouldn't have any problem finding a silent partner.

Once again I confused my dreams with reality, and the moment I approached a rich uncle for a loan, my career as a real-estate agent ended. He wouldn't invest a cent in this adventure. That evening, in a state of total drunkenness, I went to one of the rooming houses on Dorchester Boulevard and told the manager to give me the best room because I was the new owner. I showed him a copy of the lease to make him buy my story, but he didn't believe a word and told me to get out.

We started a brawl, the police intervened, accused me of "disturbing the peace" and arrested me. Once again I spent the night at Police Station no. 10 on Saint Mathieu Street.

The active phase of my alcoholism was marked by violence and often by a total loss of self-control, As I think about it, it was obvious that I was engaged in self-destruction by taking all kinds of risks, even to the point of losing my life. At 155 pounds I would always attack individuals who were bigger and heavier than I was. For the first few years, I won my fights more often than not, but later on, when alcohol had made a physical wreck out of me, I lost most of the time and only my arrogance gave me the courage to continue to take in the punches. Scars and swollen bruises were my lot; however, I remained undaunted and I stuck to my creed of: "The bigger they are, the harder they fall!"

The sickness got worse, and my physical health quickly declined. Mornings brought hallucinations and shakes to all of my extremities. Every two weeks I had to show up at the Unemployment Insurance Office to pick up my payment at the very same office where I had worked. I had to wait in line to get my unemployment check. I felt spied upon and above all judged by my former coworkers who seemed to pity me on seeing my run-down condition and my wretched appearance. Imagine! Their former president, their ex-teacher had been reduced to asking for unemployment insurance.

I felt so bad about myself that when it came time for me to sign for my check, I began to tremble so much that I couldn't do it. I had to go back to the tavern for a drink four times before I was able to rid myself of the shakes enough to write a recognizable signature on the form. Oh, God, it hurt so much to be humiliated like that. The torture of seeing my self-respect so completely crushed was almost unbearable. Where had my soul gone? Was there any hope of getting myself out of this one day? In spite of everything that had happened to me, I was incapable of admitting that I had a drinking problem, and I continued to blame life's vicissitudes, the lack of understanding of those close to me as well as the misfortune that was always dogging me.

For the umpteenth time, I called upon my mother. I asked her to convince my father to give me one last chance to get back on my feet, and I promised once again to stop drinking. My poor mother, who had become my accomplice, again succeeded in getting me back into the family. Treated like a child by my father's attitude, his angry and accusing looks, I was read the riot act: "André, I am warning you, this time it really is your last chance and, above all, don't ask me to find you a job. You have disgraced me everywhere, and I have totally lost confidence in you. You are nothing but a drunk and a liar, and you will end your days with the "rubbies"* in Viger Square."

It was obvious that I could no longer count on my father to find me a job, but I continued to use his name to get me past the doors with certain employers without his knowing it.

Between January 1961 and April 1962, I held at least six

*Drinkers of rubbing alcohol.

different jobs since I couldn't stay sober for more than a few weeks at a time.

I thought that I could escape my problems by changing job locations in a sort of "geographic cure." I made it a habit of quitting these positions just before I was about to be fired. As one could easily see, I was not making sense at all, and I was in the process of completely destroying my reputation in the workplace due to my poor attendance, my dishonesty, and my extreme insubordination, all of which were related to my problem with alcohol.

My first job was as a sales rep for an international transportation company. Barely six weeks had passed before I took off into the blue on a bender lasting several days and nights. As I was coming out of my relapse, I remembered that it was the year to celebrate my Collège de Montréal convention reunion. I decided to really do it. I was broke. That notwithstanding, I would fix it so I could have a drink on the day. At nine in the morning, I went to the Royal Embassy Hotel on Sherbrooke Street not far from the college, and I asked to see the manager, while pretending to be the president of the reunion committee. I told him that I wished to organize a celebration for the evening and that I needed a reception room as well as the hotel penthouse for the guests of honor.

The credit manager came in, asked me a few questions, and authorized my request with no more than that! I promised to pay when the banks opened, which would be after ten o'clock. So this was how I used my imagination: to make up far-fetched stories that gave me the means to get drunk without having to pay the bill. Stretched out in the big penthouse bathtub while sipping on an "Old Paar" scotch, I was already thinking of the next subterfuge that I would use to treat myself.

My mother later told me that the hotel manager (who had noted the address on my driver's license) had called her to share his indignation, saying: "Madame, in all my years as a hotel manager, I have never been so taken in and I would be ashamed to go to court if I decided to press charges against your son. I have therefore decided not to, but I would firmly warn him never to be seen in the Royal Embassy again!"

I began looking for another job, and to my great surprise, I was hired to work for the Printing Industry's Parity Committee. I held that position from March to May of 1961, and I can't even remember what my job was. Once again I had to resign because I was absent for four days straight without giving any signs of life. On the fifth day of my escapade, I contacted the manager of the Parity Committee and told him that I couldn't continue to work because I had cancer! Yea! So I was finally free from another job that was beneath me; let us therefore go and celebrate this new defeat at Cafe André.

That night, in a flight of dramatic oratory, I announced to Monique, my favorite barmaid, that I was suffering from terminal liver cancer and that I only had a few weeks to live.

With this shameless lie, I again tried to draw attention to myself, to arouse pity; what a strange way to find the love and affection that I so lacked. At the same time, I realized that I could never set foot in Café André again since I would be dead very soon and I wouldn't be able to pay off my bar tab of more than seven hundred dollars. It was the easiest way to settle this debt that was beginning to weigh heavily upon me. After all it was only a half-lie since I was really suffering from a more cunning cancer that was killing me little by little. This was the cancer of the bottle, a deadly black tumor that was spreading with impunity throughout my physical as well as spiritual being. Yes, it was the chancre of the soul. Good-bye, Café André. Good-bye, my friends in Montréal's west end. I leave for the east end where I have yet to run up any debts and where perhaps, I will finally find love and understanding.

With my drunk finished, I came home to submit to my father's latest outbursts and my mother's pleas to get help. I approached Philippe, a friend from my childhood, to find me another job. He had no idea of the extent of my drinking problem, and he found me a position as field manager in the company that he worked for, Dominion Structural Steel Ltd. specialized in the construction of skyscrapers. Afraid of heights? Not me. I was first assigned to the Toronto Dominion Bank construction project at 500 Saint Jacques Street West, in the heart of downtown, right next to Old Montréal, with all of its hotels, taverns, and clubs that invited me in around the clock.

If I didn't lose my job in the first few weeks, it was thanks to my friend Philippe. His important position in the company gave me plenty of protection. Seeing that I was incapable of resisting all the temptations of the big city, and realizing that my problem was more extreme than he first thought, Philippe arranged to have me transferred to another site. This one was far from Montréal, at Carol Lake in Labrador, where I was to be the personnel agent in charge of hiring, discipline, grievances, safety, health, and labor relations. Me, responsible for discipline? What a joke. Anyway, I had no choice, and they put me on an Air Canada "Viscount" destined for Sept-Iles where I was supposed to take a Hollinger Ungava Transport (HUT) plane to Carol Lake in Labrador. Because of bad weather, there was a low ceiling and the planes couldn't take off.

I checked in at the Hotel de Sept-Iles and began enjoying my favorite sport: boozing. I fought with everyone, I busted up the place for three days and nights. Finally they threw me and my bags out the door. On the fourth day, the weather improved and the planes could take off again for the far north. I decided to keep drinking, and I missed the plane by five minutes. The day after the downpour recommenced, and all the planes were grounded again. I called Montréal and they told me to immediately take the train to

Carol Lake, or if not, go back to Montréal. I knew for sure that if I returned to Montréal I would be fired on the spot.

I made my way to the Québec North Shore and Labrador Railway and jumped on the first train that would take me to my destination. The trip in a more than dirty passenger car took nearly two days. You could almost believe you were in the wild west of the nineteen-twenties. Montagnais Indians mixed with Blacks, Chinese, Poles, Newfies, and with a few rare Québecers. Just about everyone was either playing poker or rolling dice. There were liquor bottles everywhere, revolvers, and hunting knives hanging from the belts of half a dozen of these thugs. At last I found myself in good company!

When I arrived at Carol Lake (now called Labrador City), I was welcomed by the camp manager who showed me to my room, located in a kind of barrack infested with black flies and other insect pests. I tossed and turned all night, hardly sleeping at all. I was awakened at six o'clock for a shower, shave and breakfast. The toilets and showers were in a big tent not far from the workers' trailers. The cafeteria was in a kind of rectangular building where a thousand men could eat at the same time. Because of all the fights that broke out, the camp was segregated like the Southern United States at the beginning of the twentieth century. There the Newfies had their own trailer, separate toilets, and they went to eat at the cafeteria at different times in order to avoid any contact with the Québecers and the rest of the "White" North Americans. It was the same thing for the yellow buses that took the workers to the various work sites.

I soon made friends with the workmates who drank the most, who played bridge, and who went fishing on the unspoiled lakes in the wilderness close by. If the truth be told, I hardly worked at all. My bosses drove me crazy, because, as usual, I thought they were stupid and they didn't know anything about the work that they assigned

49

me. A week after I arrived, I became a member of the Labrador Social Club that was nothing more than a tavern where they sold such Newfoundland beers as: "Moose Head," "Black Label," "Red Label," and local moonshine. I was one of the "club's" best customers, and with my gang of Québecers, I gave a hard time to the Newfies, rain or shine. I was surrounded by giants because our employees were steel workers, riggers, and connecters and men who drove "Ukes" (giant Euclid trucks) that had tires over ten feet tall. I felt totally secure because I was protected by an army of Goliaths who really liked me since I was in a position to provide such invaluable services as pay advances, help in writing letters to their girlfriends as well as letting them use the telephone in my office to call their wives.

One day the club owner decided to increase the price of a bottle of beer by ten cents. The boys didn't appreciate the price hike, so during the night, they took apart the trailer that housed the club.

The owner had no option but to bring his price back down to what it was before, and very soon after, he was back in business. I was quite happy with life on a construction site because I hardly worked at all. I could drink any time I wanted, day or night, play cards or go fishing. On Sundays I went to a rundown chapel with a shady priest who opened up a secret room after mass where one could watch porn movies, play slot machines, have an illegal game of craps or poker and drink totally adulterated alcohol (bootleg whisky, moonshine, or Caribou).*

It was useless to add that religion became very popular there, moreover because our dear priest, our "Temple Money Lender," sold pornographic movies and magazines. Our Black Robe made so much money that he was able to roll around the site in a shiny Mercedes. What a fake, what a picture of depravity, what a cynical way had this priest

Strong Québec wine mixed with 80 proof alcohol

chosen to lead his flock astray. What little respect and faith I had for the Catholic religion had been completely wiped out. After two months of wild behavior, the boss informed me that he no longer wished to see me on the site and was sending me back to Montréal; still another who didn't understand me and who was unable to appreciate my talents. When I returned to Montréal, I was assigned to the new Place des Arts site, and I reconnected with my former buddies and the familiar flow of drinks. I was unable to work or produce any results whatsoever because I was almost always drunk. My friend Philippe didn't want to look after me anymore when he saw the size of my problem. So I was let go in August, having failed my "Geographic Cure."

Always defiant toward my employers who were working against me and who had refused to give me one last chance, I sank deeper and deeper into the evil that was gnawing at me, and I lost all hope of ever escaping. I walked down the streets of Montréal with my white construction helmet, symbol of authority on the job site, and I would criticize the appearance of the downtown buildings. In the taverns I became a construction engineer who predicted the collapse of the Stock Exchange Tower because the steel pillars came from Japan. I was becoming decidedly nonsensical, and more and more my ability to think straight was being lost in an alcoholic haze.

As luck would have it, I met a supervisor from John Colford and Sons Ltd. and I succeeded in selling him the idea that he could profit from my experience and talent. Aided by a few drinks, he saw fit to hire me as an auditor at the Place Ville Marie project. My new employer specialized in heating and air-conditioning, and all the wiring and conduits had to be installed. At that point the building of thirty some stories was nothing but bare steel girders and concrete floors. My office was on the twenty-eighth floor where there were only beams and floors without any walls or windows. I was suspended between earth and sky, and I dared not look down. I had such a fear of heights that I had to have four tumblers of vodka to give me the courage to take an open elevator up to my office. I always had a bottle hidden in my file cabinet, and I needed it after work to make it back down to the world on the ground. The feeling was overwhelming.

But the height did not prevent me from continuing to drink and to once again lose my job for the same reason. My father refused to let me stay at home, so I had to rent a room on Saint Mathieu Street near Dorchester Boulevard. I managed to survive until the Christmas holidays, thanks to my unemployment benefits and the bad checks that I kept passing in order to drink even more. Besides, due to these rubber checks and debts that I ran up in many of the clubs in Montréal's west end, I was barred from a number of places and I would soon have to go and drink in the east end where my reputation had not yet been destroyed.

Some clubs had banned me for other reasons, notably because of my verbal and physical violence, my tendency to insult those bigger and stronger than I was until all hell broke loose. One night in the Chez Paree nightclub, I picked a fight with a bouncer, and I lost all control of my anger. In less than two minutes, I threw everything I could get my hands on. I broke the big wall mirrors and many liquor bottles on the bar shelves. Four or five waiters succeeded in subduing me until the police arrived. That night I once again spent the night at Police Station number 10 on Saint Mathieu Street for disturbing the peace.

I lived more and more outside of reality and gradually strayed from the values that I had grown up with. The personalities I assumed were more unreal and weirder than ever. The stories and tangled intrigues became more and more convoluted and harder to believe. But there was always an audience for my high-quality babblings, and I took the opportunity to extol my virtues while fleeing from remorse and hiding in false illusions. Here is an example of how complex my stories were. One day at the Diana Grill, I met a tall Irish girl who fell in love with me, or rather with Captain André M. of the USAF, who I became that evening.

Hero of the Korean War, I told her stories of heart-stopping catastrophes, and I could tell by the look in her eyes how she admired me. After several very lively amorous encounters, I was already tired of her and I wanted to break it off. What would be easier for me than to resort to lying and tell her that I was off to Vietnam? I showed her a fake telegram that I had sent myself. She was saddened by my sudden departure.

A few weeks later in my alcoholic madness, I sent another telegram to the Diana Grill's manager that said that I had disappeared or died in combat. I was dead. And so my Irish Mary would forget me and I would be rid of her for good. There it was, with my temporary insanity and my frequent blackouts, I soon forgot that I was in Vietnam, declared missing and presumed dead. So I showed up at the Diana Grill a month later, and when Mary saw me, she became completely pale, stood up and cried out: "André? Captain André, I thought you were dead! Oh my God, is that really you?" Then she fainted and fell to the floor.

I took off as fast as my legs could carry me. I never saw Mary, nor set foot in that place again. Insanity was worming its way into my spirit. Madness was gaining ground and despair was taking possession of my soul.

Where can I find the courage to end this once and for all? How can I rid myself of these sickening fears, this devouring depression? This time despair is rooted and strong enough for me to dream again of suicide. Ah, yes. There's a gas stove in my room. It's a soft and easy death, a sleep in which this thirst is gone forever.

However, the holidays were fast approaching, and it wasn't the proper time to kill myself and ruin the family celebration. Oh, well. After New Year's, I can leave in peace after having seen my family one last time. During this period of joblessness and vagrancy, I drank constantly and my physical and mental health rapidly deteriorated; my blackouts were more frequent and I often woke up in the morning with cuts and bruises on my face, body, and hands without knowing where they had come from. Had I been beaten up again? Had I seriously hurt someone? Where had I been last night? All these questions remained unanswered, and they plunged me into deep anguish and distress. I experienced a feeling of powerlessness such that I melted into tears and I endured an indefinable pain.

I can't find the right words to describe this misery in my soul, this deep self-loathing. Lord, I am so sad and desperate. About a week before New Year's, I decided to call my mother to wish her a Merry Christmas and to ask her whether I could celebrate New Year's at home like we had always done. To my great astonishment, my mother let me know that the house was closed to me. Even if I had always been welcomed to family celebrations in the past, my father had decided to end all contact with his eldest son, once and for all, and to banish him forever. I knew that I didn't deserve any pity and that my father was absolutely right to try to stop me from continuing to dishonor the whole family. That same day I decided to put an end to my life since I had now been totally rejected, even by my father and by my mother who loved me so. I was hurt and wanted to revenge this deep wound to my pride. I would turn on the taps of my gas stove on New Year's Day itself!

But before ending it all, I wanted to see again the woman whom I loved so, the one whom I had ridiculed. I wanted to say good-bye to Claudette and to tell her one last time that she was the only one I had really ever loved. I wanted to ask her to forgive me, to explain my chaotic existence to her and to thank her for the perfect love that she had inspired in me from the first instant when we met. No, I couldn't leave this cursed earth that had given me less than nothing without again seeing the love in Claudette's pure heart and the heaven in her eyes.

With this thought only, I felt a sort of calm welling up in me and a hint of interior peace, like a salve on the open wounds of my deep hurt and despair. In my alcoholic haze, my clouded mind neglected the fact that Claudette was about to be married to another man and that she could never be mine. Despite this situation, I had the audacity to ask Claudette to come and help me. I got in touch with her on New Year's Eve, and I begged her to come to Montréal. As incredible as it seemed, she took the train from Lachute on New Year's Day after having informed her future husband and showed up in Montréal to come and comfort me. Her intuition as well as her instinct made her feel that the situation was urgent. The fire of spiritual love that has always consumed us has never gone out and will always keep smouldering.

Without knowing it, Claudette had saved my life, as if maybe one day our love might be reborn and miraculously burn anew. I was so happy to see her again, and I said to myself that perhaps the day would come when in another life, we could, both of us, make our ideal love come true in an unknown dimension. This dream encouraged me to stay alive and postpone my attempt at suicide for another day. After all, I was still able to find another job. And, who knows, I might be able to better control my demonic drinking?

I applied for the position of Field Auditor with a company in Wabush. I got the job after having lied copiously during the interview about my ability in accounting and auditing. There I was again, hired for a position for which I had neither experience nor competence. So I took advantage of the fact that the company had an urgent need and hadn't taken the trouble to verify my curriculum vitae. I told my mother that I was off to Labrador and, against my father's wishes, she packed me a suitcase full of clean clothes and gave me a small sum of money to tide me over to my first pay check.

On February 26th, 1962, I landed at Wabush Lake in Labrador, and I was welcomed by the site manager who took me to dinner at the "white helmet" cafeteria where all the management personnel ate. I was very happy to see that they didn't sell alcohol, which helped me to stay dry for some time. As opposed to Labrador City, where we lived in tents, I found myself in a brand new staff house with a private bath and a games room in the basement.

I often thought of Claudette, who had saved my life a few weeks before, and I decided to write to her. I knew that she should be married soon, and that by my fault, I had lost all hope of holding on to her love. Nevertheless, I tried desperately to stay connected to her so we could at least remain friends. Here is the complete text of that letter:

Wabush Lake, Labrador, April 6th, 1962,

Dear Claudette,

As I promised; and on behalf of the captivating friendship which has joined and sustained us through the dark times in our life, I take this opportunity to send you my news.

First off, I had a fine trip on board the company plane and I landed in Wabush about noon on the 26th of February. The bright sun and the magnificent mountains greeted me with a smile, and I feel at home despite the 48 below zero temperature.

As you should know, in my situation, solitude is easier to endure in God's country than in the Devil's playground, Montréal. I find in these lakes, mountains and wild animals an asylum and a sort of revival that I could never find in Montréal. I wouldn't say that I am living the life of a hermit, because in spite of everything, my still joyful attitude won't let me, but I am leading my tastes and my pastimes in a more natural direction, which pleases me greatly.

No, I haven't forgotten romance completely, not at all! I

can still get the feeling when I listen to Pat Boone sing "Love Letters in the Sand"!

Because it is so difficult for our religion to permit another spouse, I am finding the necessary solitude here to try and deeply understand my situation and to find a healthy answer before God and humanity!

I am very pleased to see that your happiness soon awaits you and I wish you all the joy that you so much deserve. Besides, with your gifts I am sure that you will reach the heights of love and that you will be fed by the highest feelings throughout your life.

I still have the picture on my desk that we had taken at Ruby Foo's, (Ah! The good times we had!) and that comforts me to know that you are still there (even 1,000 miles away) and the memory of our deep friendship warms my heart. . . .

I sincerely hope to hear from you, even if it only be a short letter. This would please me very much and I would so thank you.

Good night, Claudette.

Your friend André xx (friendship)

I reread the letter, and with a tortured heart and death in my soul, I sent it to Lachute as soon as I could.

I socialized with two accountants (real ones, they were), and they asked me to play bridge with them. About a week after I arrived, they showed up with their bottles of scotch, rye, and vodka. I resisted temptation the first night and I excused myself by pretending to have a stomach ache. But on the second evening, I could no longer hold myself back, and I bought one bottle of rye and one of vodka. That was the end of my period of abstinence. As of that evening, I fell back into the habit of drinking every day.

My work consisted of auditing the books of the subcontractors working on the site in order to avoid accounting fraud and to more tightly control expenses. Like most alcoholics, I quickly learned my new profession and was able to do all my work in the space of two hours per day. The rest of the time was devoted to drinking and playing cards with my coworkers. With a schedule like that, I became quite physically ill again, and the morning shakes came back along with the nightmares and the episodes of delirium. I neglected my work and attracted the reprimands of my superiors. To make matters worse, a new bar opened a week later. I became the best customer at Wabush's Sir Grenfeld Hotel. It was only a question of days before totally descending into the implacable whirlpool of my thirst and my constant obsession with drink.

In a last desperate effort, I managed to stop drinking for two days in a row, and I tried to verify the books of the site cafeteria and store management subcontractor. I thought that I had discovered a fraud of over two million dollars, and I immediately reported this to my boss who asked me to keep this under wraps. Strangely enough, the whole affair was covered up, and I found out that the presumed culprit was the Big Boss's son, a multimillionaire who was able to buy the confidentiality of his managers, and in so doing, to clear his son of the fraud that he had committed. But I wasn't for sale, and I shouted to anyone at the hotel who would listen that the boss's son was nothing but a crook.

Forty-eight hours later, the Mounties (RCMP) escorted me under guard to the company plane, and I was unceremoniously transferred to the Montréal head office. That was the end of another job. I was fired on the spot for disclosing an affair that I should have kept confidential. My overzealousness and my arrogance had brought me down once more. When would I learn to be more careful? Back in Montréal again, with nowhere to go. My parents agreed to take me in once more on a temporary basis.

After two months without work, I succeeded in ferreting out a job in a hardware store on Craig Street where I was the assistant manager of the precision tools section. This time I was able to stay sober for close to two months, but I had a lot of trouble controlling my desire to renew my drinking. In addition I had a hard time accepting such a boring job, and my pride suffered whenever I had to clean the counters or sweep the floor. In my third month on the job, a young cashier caught my attention and we became friends; she confided to me that she was pregnant and that the father of the child wanted nothing more to do with her.

In a spirit of (interested) generosity, I offered to take care of her and her coming child, and I made a date so we could discuss this further. We were to meet at eight in the evening at the "Press Club" on Saint Denis Street. Arriving a bit early, I asked the waiter to get me a soft drink. I sipped this sugar water while thinking that once again I could leave home by pretending to be the loving savior of a woman with whom I could finally lead a normal life.

An hour had already gone by, and she still hadn't arrived for our meeting. I phoned her at her place and asked her what had happened. She told me that she had changed her mind and didn't want to see me any more! I was disappointed, insulted, and brought down. How could a woman refuse such a chivalrous offer, such a selfless act of charity? It was inconceivable! I called out: "Waiter, bring me three beers and a Marie Brizard anisette."

It had begun again, I took my first glass. It was the beginning of another episode of my non-life. That night I didn't go home because I was too drunk to endure the paternal fireworks or my mother's sadness. In the morning I awoke with the horror of my relapse, and I stayed away from work.

When I showed up three days later, the manager confronted me and threatened to have me fired. Still slightly inebriated and in a bad mood because of my relapse, I came back at him: "Don't take the trouble to fire me. I only came back to give my resignation."

And while I was there, why not blow off some steam? In a biting tone, I began to rant against all the store owners who abused their employees by forcing poor working conditions on them, these millionaires who get rich off the backs of their workers.

"Anyway, I am here to convince your slaves to demand to be accredited and to form a union, so they can get some respect. You are nothing but outdated abusers and incompetents."

The litany continued until the manager threatened to call the police. I left the store still shouting and headed to the nearest tavern.

On the street for the sixth time in the last two years, I felt that soon I wouldn't be able to work at all and that I would inevitably lose all credibility with any potential employers. What little money I had left allowed me to continue drinking while wandering from one rooming house to another. I hardly ate anything. I lost a lot of weight. My hallucinations became more frequent and more violent. I noticed that my rationality was vacillating and soon madness would take over. In spite of everything, I kept trying to find work, and I would check the classified ads in the newspapers; not having a fixed address, I used that of my parents, and in December, my mother let me know that I had received a letter from the federal government. I hurried home and opened the letter. My application had been accepted to fill the position of employment officer in the Unemployment Insurance Office in Lachute.

Unbelievable! The recruiter had surely not done his work properly, because if he had checked my job record only a little, he would have discovered that my dossier at the Montréal Unemployment Insurance Office was not outstanding. But I certainly wasn't about to tell him, above all because this appointment would take me to Lachute, the very town where my beloved Claudette still lived. Could I see her again, if only for a brief moment? Could I get to meet her once again? In my fevered mind, I played out all sorts of scenarios, each one more optimistic than the last, even though she had just gotten married.

My father let me come home for a few days, to give me time to get my health back a little, before I left for Lachute. This short period of forced abstinence gave me back a bit of physical strength, but it didn't help me to forget my implacable obsession with alcohol. It raised other hopes in my mother, who thought that this time would be it. She bought what was needed, packed my suitcases, again lent me money, and wished me good luck. According to my father, nothing good would come of it, and he predicted that, alone, in a town like Lachute, I would not be able to resist temptation for long. The past guaranteed the future, and once a drunk, blah, blah, blah. And he was absolutely right. He knew his drunk of a son well, having seen him wreck the chances that he was given many times.

"No, André," he said to me, "I can't believe your new promise. You always drink. You have no will to change your life. You have no backbone, and like a slug, you'll crawl 'til you die." For me it was not a question of will, but of my total inability to halt the advance of my sickness.

On January the 2nd, 1963, I got off the train in Lachute and made my way to the Hotel Laurentien to rent a room while waiting to find something better the moment when I had my first paycheck. I knew my way around from the time I went out with Claudette in 1957. I would often go to the local hotels after carefully dropping her off at her place, to hide the fact that I was a very heavy drinker. I therefore made the rounds of the hotels to pompously announce my arrival and my new position at the Lachute Unemployment Insurance Office. I also did it to find out if Claudette was around and whether her brother still lived there. I wanted to reestablish my contact with her. Even if she was newly married and seemingly happy, I couldn't forget her. I still loved her, I would always love her, and I kept drinking to feed my illusions and embellish my dreams with even more unreality.

Then it's last call. I'm totally drunk and, painfully, I find my way back to my hotel to get a few hours sleep before going to the office for the first time. It's two in the morning, and I pass out in my bed, carried into a sleep interrupted by hallucinations.

At four in the morning, I awoke with a start. Someone was violently banging on my door.

"It's the police! Open the door immediately or we'll break it down!"

They didn't wait for me to answer and burst into my room. They were three hulks. One of them grabbed me in a bear hug, another handcuffed me behind my back, while the third quickly and brutally went through my personal effects. I did a good job telling them that I hadn't done anything, but they didn't stop until they noticed my passport and my letter of appointment from the federal government. I was damn scared! They quickly apologized by explaining that it was a case of "mistaken identity" and that I was in the room registered to someone named Reeves, who was wanted for the murder of a police officer.

Those detectives were so nervous and aggressive that it would have been all over for me if I had made the slightest move to fight back. For those who remember the event, Reeves was Marcotte's accomplice. Marcotte was dressed up as Santa Claus for a holdup in Ville-Saint-Laurent, which resulted in the death of a police officer. The "Santa Claus Marcotte" affair was reported in all the papers at the time, and Reeves had hidden out in Lachute until New Year's Day. The day after, without knowing it, I rented the room that he was in the night before. On the bright side, the night's traumatic events sobered me up immediately, so I was in relatively good shape when I went to work the next morning.

The office manager welcomed me politely and introduced me to the employees. From my elevated point of view, I could already see that they were mostly incompetent because none of them were university graduates. I thought to myself that the manager feared for his job when faced with my vast experience. I was off to a good start anyway, but I couldn't concentrate on my work for very long. I had only three ideas on my mind: number one, reestablish relations with Claudette; number two, get myself involved in the upcoming federal election; and number three, find a way to get out of the office as much as possible in order to have more time to drink and to show the Lachute folks what I was made of. I informed my manager that I had to visit all the employers in the region to sell them on the services provided by our office.

My work plan was accepted, and so I was free to bar hop and join the clique. I drank every day and proclaimed to anyone who would listen that I was a secret political organizer for "The Federal Liberal Party." Again I resorted to my telegram trick and sent messages left and right to selected candidates and their campaign organizers. I shot off my mouth in all the bars and hotels proclaiming that the Conservatives were no good, and I passed judgment on important people in the region. Once again I took on adversaries more powerful than I was, and I irritated them so much that they sent their enforcers and the local police after me.

I was in the office about one day a week to verify the new requests for benefits and interview particular candidates for available positions. I ran across this weird case while checking a request for benefits. On his benefit file under job search, a so-called Lucien pretended that he had been a lion tamer, hoping that he would never be offered a job and so collect the maximum unemployment insurance benefits.

I called the poor guy to my office for an interview at the time when the touring Barnum and Bailey Circus was setting up in Montréal. When Lucien showed up, I showed him a request from Barnum and Bailey for a lion tamer, and I offered him the job. Actually, I had faked the request form in order to really teach the little crook a lesson that he couldn't steal from the government while I was around. Totally shame-faced, Lucien mumbled: "I haven't tamed any animals for a long time. I can't take the job."

I answered him back in my best and most triumphant bureaucratic tone: "So, my dear sir, if you refuse this job, I will disqualify you, I will cut off your benefits immediately, and I will reclaim all prior monies you received under false pretenses as a lion tamer."

What a great way to be popular in a town you have just arrived in! That night, at the Hotel Chevrier tavern, Lucien was waiting for me with his gang and I was under no illusions as to their intentions. They were four giants, and I had no chance of winning such an unfair fight with the odds so stacked against me.

I had to swallow my pride and quickly find a way out: "Hey, guys! It's my turn to buy a round. I hope Lucien has a sense of humor because I really had him going today!"

Within a few seconds, those menacing stares had turned into bursts of laughter and Lucien put me in a head-lock: "Damn, you really had me! So it's true, you aren't going to cut my benefits after all?"

Whew! I had just saved myself from a real beating. Recently I had lost most of my fights, and I was aware that my boxing skills were decreasing. Ah, if only I could take them on one at a time. Maybe one day I would meet only one of them, and who knows, I might get my own back?

After three weeks I had run out of cash to pay for my room, having spent all the money that my mother had advanced me.

As well, it seemed that there was a mix-up in the pay system in Ottawa and I had not received my salary by the expected date. The Hotel Laurentien refused me credit, which forced me to move my stock to the Windsor Hotel where my credit was still good because I often drank with the owner. By chance it was conveniently located less than a hundred yards from my office.

My mother agreed to lend me two-hundred dollars more to help me make it to my first paycheck while warning me that it was the last time that she could help me out. This new cash allowed me to carry on my career as an "undercover" organizer for the Liberal Party of Canada, to get myself deeper and deeper into trouble and to really aggravate the influential people in the county.

But across the confused maze of my acts and intentions, the image of Claudette regularly reappeared, and in the evenings whenever I was perched at the hotel bar, I heard music that reminded me of the sweet memory of my only, and still living, love. I cried into my glass. I raged over the destruction of the best thing that had ever happened in my life. I made one last try to see her. I asked her brother, Guy, whom I had met at the hotel, to be my intermediary and to give her a message. I sent her the picture taken at Ruby Foo's in 1957, at a time when our love seemed to offer all the hope in the world. By cruelly reminding her of this wonderful moment, I believed that she would give in and agree to see me despite the fact that she was recently married. How rude! How self-centered! Who the hell did I think I was?

How could Claudette agree to meet me after all the hurt I had caused her? How could she understand and believe in my love after I had so greatly disappointed her? She was right to refuse my request, and her brother informed me that she had no wish to see me again. He returned my records of the singer Yma Sumac, the Inca princess, that I had given to Claudette as a present and asked me to stop bothering her. I drank all night to drown my pain, and the bottle was my daily companion more and more. It was my partner in crime for all my stupid actions, the mistress of my nightmares, the one that inspired all my projects and the guardian of all my hate, all my resentment, all my pain, and the source of my systematic self-destruction.

I was heartsick after Claudette refused me (with reason). I could no longer see clearly through the chaos of my thoughts and the incoherence of my mind. I then decided to take out my spite and my anger on whomever came my way. I would pick a fight with someone at the bar whom I would choose for no apparent reason. The next morning, sitting in the same bar, I saw a man with a swollen face and two black eyes, and a drink in his shaky hand.

As soon as he saw me, he put down his glass and quickly made for the door. I couldn't remember having seen the guy before. However from the barmaid, I learned that I had beaten this man within an inch of his life the night before, and if it had not been for three other men who managed to hold me down, I would probably have killed him. Was it possible? That man, a lumberjack, surely a lot stronger than I was, was unable to stand up to my unbridled savagery and took off when he saw me. I had reached a level of dementia where I couldn't even remember what I had done, I had become this wild madman who had lost all control of his emotions.

At the beginning of May 1963, I still hadn't received my first paycheck and I had run out of money, but the hotel let me run up my bill for a bit longer, which allowed me to continue my make-believe electoral campaign and so scared the establishment that the police got involved and ordered me to leave the town of Lachute within forty-eight hours!

I sent them packing and dared them to issue a warrant. I began to throw bottles, glasses and anything else I could find, which was what they were waiting for in order to arrest me, handcuff me, and take me to the town police station. Once I was calmed down and sobered up a bit, but still handcuffed, the chief of police directed me into a cell after the official body search.

I became very aggressive and shouted at him: "If you lock me in this cell, I will come back and kill you as soon as I get out. Understand?"

I appeared to have scared him enough, since the cell door stayed open.

To avoid staying overnight at the police station, I called a friend who was a judge in Saint-Jerome, and he was able to have me released during the afternoon on the condition that I kept the peace. I had forty-eight hours to leave town. There were only twenty-four left. Time to resign my job in the morning and to hide out in the Hotel Hebert in Ayersville near Lachute.

During the evening I started my stupid intrigues again, thinking I was safe in a suburb of Lachute. At nine o'clock the following morning, the door to my room was forced open by a "Provincial" policeman, who was accompanied by a detective and a "Federal" agent. There were three of them to read me my rights. They ordered me to leave town and the surrounding area immediately or be arrested and accused of uttering death threats to a police officer.

I had no choice. I had lost my job again. I was ridiculed to the point of being kicked out of town. I had failed to meet with my love. There was nothing left for me to do there. Once outside, the police drove me to the city limits on, what was then, Highway 8. I asked them to send me a taxicab. Ten minutes later I was on my way to Montréal where a far more uncertain destiny awaited me. I was afraid, very afraid. Despair overran me.

It was the point of no return.

4

Hell Bound

Back in Montréal, armed with my ever-present NSF check book, I stayed at Motel Pierre in Ville Saint-Laurent after getting loaded at the Texas Tavern. It was March 10th, 1963; the day before my thirty-third birthday. Sly as a fox, I knew that my parents could not stop me from coming home on my birthday, so I called my mother to tell her that I was returning to the fold following my resignation from my job in Lachute due to some personality conflicts with my superior. I asked my father to put up with me for a short time since I was not intending to accept his hospitality for long. Actually, my forced abstinence couldn't last for more than a few weeks at a time. This damned obsession to take a drink was haunting me relentlessly.

With great difficulty I succeeded in finding what appeared to be my last decent job by falsifying my curriculum vitae and deliberately lying during the interview as well. It was now the beginning of May. I had not taken a drink for almost five weeks, and in my mind, a slim hope was reborn, since, once again, I had a chance to recover. Unfortunately it was only a mirage, and I couldn't keep it up for long. I did well the first week, but at the same time, I learned that I would be getting my first paycheck the following Thursday. The simple fact of knowing that I would soon have money awakened within me an irresistible urge to take off again, and my sick mind was already planning the itinerary for my next drunk. As if this were not already enough, I finally received the money for the nine weeks of "work" in Lachute that Ottawa owed me! At last I was glory bound again and ready to satisfy my inexhaustible need to build up my ego with new impostures.

The fatal day arrived, and at exactly five o'clock, the taxi was waiting at the office door to take me on a trip to those rare clubs where I was still tolerated. Having almost nine hundred dollars to spend made me quickly lose control, and I drank until I passed out. The next morning at ten, I woke up with a start. I could remember nothing except that I had to call in "sick" at the office in order to save my job. In a state of fear and panic, I avoided talking with my boss and left the message with the receptionist. Whew, I was saved, freed for the weekend, which would allow me to finish my bender and recover by the time I had to go to work on Monday morning. Dream on! I still didn't understand that a single drink was too much for me and a thousand drinks were not enough; I had come to that point in my sickness where I began to drink every day, all day, without stopping for years, en route to my complete destruction.

On Friday afternoon I left for Lachute possibly to see Claudette, whose face was seemingly unwilling to leave my thoughts. But once there I made no effort to find her because I knew that if she saw me drunk like that, she would shut me out of her heart forever. The very thought that I should forget her offended me and plunged me into the pain of deep despair, giving me more reason to drink and feel sorry for myself. I drank so much that I lost all sense of time, and I came to the following Tuesday. I panicked. What excuse could I offer to explain my absence this time? I made up a story and said that my car had had a major breakdown, which prevented me coming in to work before Thursday. The moment I hung up, I remembered that before leaving, I had posted a notice on the company bulletin board asking that someone give me a ride to work because I didn't have a car. Big mistake, I had really blown it this time! What a dumb excuse to invent mechanical problems for a car that I didn't have!

I took a taxi from Lachute to Montréal, and to avoid my father's usual complaining, I arrived home before he came back from work. My mother handed me a telegram, which read as follows: "Your services are no longer required by this company. Signed William L. Vice President." My last job had only lasted nine days. I blamed my dismissal on my habitual bad luck. In spite of everything that had happened I couldn't recognize and acknowledge that I had a serious drinking problem. I told my mother that I was leaving home for good, and I promised that one day I would pay back all the money that she had lent me as well as all the NSF checks she had covered to keep me from going to jail.

Still under the effects of my morning drinking, I left quickly before my father could arrive. My mother's sad and troubled expression left me heartsick and filled me with sorrow. I jumped into a taxi, and led by my thirst, the slave I had become said to the driver: "Take me to the Cafe Saint-Jacques please."

Because I had been "fasting" for about six hours, I was shaking a lot and it was only by using both hands that I was able to down my drink. It was hell that had begun to show itself. The vicious circle of obsession, thirst, and remorse dominated everything else. I could only be stopped when the clubs and blind pigs* were closed. It was almost daybreak when I would collapse onto a flimsy cot in a second-rate tourist room. The gray days had come. My heart and soul were frozen. I had succeeded in emptying my life of anyone who cared about me, and I would be alone with my misery.

I went looking for a room that I could rent by the week. I found what I wanted on Saint-Christophe near Ontario

*Illegal after-hours bars

Street. The room was large enough with a gas stove and a refrigerator in the hallway that I shared with the other tenants. This was living! The landlady really liked me and let me have this fine abode for only twelve dollars a week. Being on unemployment insurance allowed me to pay the rent, all the while saving the rest of my money for drinking as well as eating occasionally . . . very occasionally. It didn't take me long to move in as the contents of my suitcase barely filled one dresser drawer and a shelf in the bathroom for my two towels, a razor, soap, toothbrush, and my "Aqua Velva" after-shave lotion. I paid for two weeks in advance and then went out to find the nearest liquor outlets. There were at least a dozen taverns and another ten clubs within walking distance.

I chose the Milano Tavern at the corner of Ontario and Saint-Timothée Streets because its clients were people like me, out of money, living from day to day, without the will to change or the hope of doing so. Together we could judge society, put down religion, curse the rich and the politicians, and feel sorry for ourselves together in our unhappiness, misfortune, misery, and our near-total isolation. I had found soul mates at last with whom I shared a common language, one without hope for life, in search of the only freedom possible, which made us suffer the most because, uncontrolled, it led to the death of the soul. There I had found the total freedom to destroy all facets of my life: physical, moral, spiritual, emotional, family and professional.

Even if I was now in the very modest surroundings of Montréal's east end, my pride was always ever-present and I wanted to keep astonishing those around me by inventing other personalities that would draw the attention of my new audience. It was quite evident that I had to adapt myself to a class of people from a very different "culture" from the middle class, of west Montréal. I certainly couldn't pass myself off as a doctor or other professional at the Milano Tavern. I had to make up a hero who was at once striking, fabulous, and fantastic in order to excite the less lively imagination of my future friends who were the "pillars" of this community.

So why not pretend to be a native Indian? I was pleased with the idea, and I had only to put all my creative ingenuity to the task to make up an original character that would intrigue the most cynical and amaze the most gullible. Since I had read a lot of books about adventures in the land of the Incas and knew about the exotic and sensational singer Yma Sumac, I decided to become her nephew by naming myself Aner (André) Sumac, prince of the Incas. Taking inspiration from the costumes, jewelry, and poses of my "aunt" Yma, I dressed myself by imitating her photos on her record covers as closely as possible. To make my undertaking even more believable, I became friends with a real Mohawk Indian who helped me perfect my costume (a sort of skirt or kilt), a multicolor body make-up and with the help of old tin cans, oyster shells (and whatever else), pendants and bracelets that I wore around my neck, arms, and ankles. The whole thing was so well done that I almost believed it myself!

Dressed like that I went out on the street with my chance companion and resolutely made my way toward the Milano Tavern to make my "premiere" appearance. It was three-thirty in the afternoon, and the children, just getting out of school, followed us along the sidewalk, admiring my costume and the dance steps I made to the imaginary Quechua music playing in my head. The traffic slowed, horns tooted, policemen, smiled and people on the street looked at each other in disbelief!

During the short periods of lucidity, which occasionally came to me, I fearfully realized that my rationality was in the process of completely leaving me. I was rapidly sinking beneath the waves of insanity without a life jacket to save me from that terrible nightmare. Yes, I had really gone over the edge, and my weird behavior was becoming worse.

In the tavern some guys made fun of me a little, but those who were more afraid pretended to believe me because they didn't doubt that I could be violent, especially with a twenty-inch machete hanging from the belt of my kilt. As unpredictable as I was, I might decide to take on the "white" enemy at any moment. But the alcohol helped to change it all into a pretense of feigned amusement, and almost dead-drunk, I went dancing into the street on the way back to my room. Falling occasionally on all fours, I ended up hurting myself in a few places, and I made it to my room all bloody and bruised. My friend Pete the Mohawk looked after me and bandaged me up. I blacked out and fell into a sleep scattered with a haze of ethyletic hallucinations.

This "Inca Celebration" would last for three or four months, enough time to use up my unemployment insurance benefits and to leave me incapable of paying my room rent. During this time I did nothing but drink and drink again, day after day, week after week, often around the clock. How was it that one's body could take such punishment? I still ask that myself today, whenever I think of those things that I did to my poor carcass for all those years. When I awoke I always tried to have some alcohol by my side to "recover" from my overconsumption of the night before and, as long as I had a bit of money, I permitted myself this luxury and made my shakes go away, but this was not always the case.

Often, whenever I was broke, the tavern manager would ask me to take out the garbage in exchange for ten glasses of beer (a dollar's worth in 1964), which served as a remedy to make my "morning shakes" disappear. This would soon become my morning ritual since I no longer had any money to buy my first drinks. My other problem was that I was incapable of holding a glass due to my shakes. I was then reduced to asking help from "Tonton," a tavern regular. He would go with me to the rest room where I would sit down on one of the toilets while he emptied the ten glasses, one after the other, into my gullet. After having been stuffed like this, I could finally hold a bottle in my two hands and undertake another day of drinking. In the future this morning ritual would become a daily one.

During my "weird Inca" period, I became more and more incoherent and my strange behavior became more extreme. The sun being the God of the Incas, I often went up on the rooming house roof to worship this god dressed only in my fake hardware. The neighbors were offended by my nakedness, and they warned my landlady to stop letting me go up on the roof; otherwise they would call the police. I should therefore cease the practice of my "religion" to avoid a scandal and eviction from my room. But I thought I looked so good in my Inca costume that I decided to get my picture taken in that outfit to immortalize the character I had become. I managed to keep one of these pictures, and I will mention it again in another chapter. Amusing to begin with, this character quickly began to pale and, after three months of use, the regulars of the neighborhood tavern had lost all interest in Aner Sumac, Prince of the Incas. So gradually I let my costume's finery and feathers fall away and became a plain white "civilian" once again.

My landlady, who soon realized that I had a very serious drinking problem decided to send me a "savior" personified by a member of Alcoholics Anonymous. This good Samaritan showed up at my door one morning and insisted that he talk with me in order to convince me to join his AA group. I was in no mood to listen. I told him to get lost. I grabbed my machete in a threatening manner and began swearing at him. When I sprang toward him, he hightailed it out of there, and I chased him down the street until he jumped into a taxi and managed to escape my insane furor. Back in my room, utterly worn out and exhausted by this frantic chase, I threw myself onto my cot, crying with rage and despair because I now knew that I was totally owned by alcohol and, one by one, my lives were being destroyed without my being able to do a thing about it.

My physical health was deteriorating. I was so thin that it frightened me. My vital organs were showing signs of weakness, and blackouts and memory losses increased. All of this was inexorably destroying my physical life. As far as my professional life was concerned, it had been thoroughly obliterated for some time and my spiritual life had disappeared the day I became perfect enough to be God's equal as I replaced Him. I also had no emotional life, having systematically built a void around me by excluding anyone who really loved me.

Every good thing has to come to an end. My unemployment insurance benefits had stopped, and I could no longer pay the rent. When I told my landlady, she offered to let me keep my room for a while longer. I thanked her and said to her: "You should know, my dear lady, that I am an honorable man and the moment I can't pay my rent, I will give you back the keys."

Was I still so proud even when I was in such dire straits? That's for sure, because a week later I deserted my room and left my Indian friend to fend for himself. I later learned that my landlady was herself an alcoholic, who had found the way to sobriety by joining A.A., from whence came her interest in my "case" and the sending of a group member to "convert" me. I also found out that she had contacted my mother, telling her the sorry state that I was in and how badly I would end up if I continued to weaken as I did.

At the Milano Tavern, I hung out with a group of "flyer guys"* who drank almost as much as I did. The fact that I was in such a select company of bums stood me well in my

*Advertising circulars delivery men

present circumstances. One day the circular-delivery boss offered me a day's work at a dollar an hour. I said yes right away to get a few dollars for beer. The day ended, we returned to the tavern for "supper," which consisted of a small glass of oysters for forty cents, a cube of strong cheese for ten cents, and ten glasses of draft beer at ten cents apiece. Having no fixed address, I did as the others and made a habit of sleeping at a flop house* on De Vitré Street. These shelters for "rubbies" and other homeless men were located in a neighborhood full of rundown and abandoned houses. Hard times became harder, I could feel them breathing down my neck.

My circular-delivery job kept me busy for three or four hours a day every week, but it was not enough to slake my constant thirst.

Often when night came, I didn't have the fifty cents needed to pay for a bed at the shelter, and I had to sleep outside in an abandoned vehicle or unlocked car. As a matter of fact, I hated sleeping at the "flop" because I would wake up all dirty and whenever I saw the poor slobs around me, I would almost throw up and feel sick to my stomach for the rest of the morning. Yet I was one of them, neither better nor worse, in the process of losing what little remaining dignity I had.

I often met my new friends in the alleys near the tavern, and, lacking good alcohol, we would concoct cocktails that could very well blind or poison us. These mixtures of wood alcohol, alcohol-based lotions, melted shoe polish, and the dregs of bottles found in the garbage or stolen from somewhere now served as a remedy and "tonic" for a successful undertaking of the new day that offered itself to us. This hellish diet intensified the decline in my physical and mental health. I weighed less than one hundred and thirty pounds. I was bruised all over from falling so often while

*Shelter for the homeless

losing my balance or blacking out. I felt my strength leaving me, and I often became delirious in a sleep shot through with horrible and frightening visions. Often I thought that it was going to be my last night on earth and that death was finally coming to save me from my torture. But I imagined that if I was still alive, it was because even God didn't want me and that I was condemned to atone for all my shameful sins on this damned planet earth that had only ever given me grief.

Having run out of other options, I became an accomplice to the petty thieves who shared the tavern with us. Some of them stole checks from mailboxes and often had me cash them at a local bank or business where my "commission" would average out at around 10 percent. They knew when they came to me that I would do anything for a drink and that I was ready to take on a bank manager or any other sucker to get what I wanted. These little fraud operations sometimes yielded significant results, but no matter what the amount, I always found a way to spend it all by buying rounds for my family of vagrants and paying off my debt to the bartender.

This scheme came just in time since I had lost my circular-delivery job due to "physical incapacitation." I was so weak that I was barely able to carry the heavy sack while walking more than a mile and also climbing stairs in order to deliver the circulars. One day, unable to go on, I dumped half my load by putting a stack of those damn papers down a sewer. After that I delivered the rest by folding them together and throwing them up to the doors on the upper floors to avoid going up the stairs. The inspector caught me, and I was fired on the spot.

In spite of my weakness, pride always drove me on, so I would try to pick a fight with anyone who dared look at me too long, acted superior, or even disagreed with me; I who was always right and so splendid in my frayed and faded rags. This state of mind would lead me into a number of mishaps where my life itself would be endangered.

Every time I came into a little money I would venture downtown. I would leave the protective cocoon of my little gang of tavern buddies at the Milano to go and spit my vengeful venom into the face of imagined new enemies. On a May afternoon, I went down to the "Quartier Français" Tavern on Saint-Hubert Street and I sat down not far from a group of blowhards wearing black "Chevaliers de l'independance"* sweaters. Even though I was alone, I was bold enough to look down on them from the height of my impertinence and aggressively and pointedly, I began attacking their political platform even though the subject barely interested me. The waiter begged me to keep quiet, to no avail, and I kept insulting them and treating them like losers and idiots. The waiter ordered me to change tables and placed me at the front next to the exit. That only encouraged me to shout louder so they could still hear me, up until the point when I was hustled out the door.

Upon leaving the tavern, I staggered toward Saint-Catherine Street, with the "Chevaliers" running after me. They caught up with me in front of the Da Giovani Restaurant, and they started to beat me up. Now there were four of them on me, I protected my head, their punches raining down on me, I fell face down on the sidewalk. I was kicked in the stomach, ribs, back and legs. I felt my bladder and my intestines empty into my pants. No one stopped or wanted to get involved, not even the cop who just kept on directing the traffic. While semiconscious I felt myself being lifted up and thrown into the air, then everything went dark. I came to at the bottom of a pit on the Berri-Demontigny subway construction site.

More dead than alive, having tumbled down a steep grade ending in mud and stones a hundred feet below, I regained consciousness a bit at a time and woke up dirty

*Knights of Independence

and bloody with torn and excrement-filled clothing. I painfully began the hard climb back up where I would have to hop the security fence that I had been thrown over. After struggling for half an hour, I reached the top under the disdainful gazes of the passersby who made wide detours around me. I steered myself to a tavern mate's place whose digs were about a mile and a half away on Jeanne-Mance Street.

My friend "Blackie," who had recently gotten out of jail for attempted murder, couldn't believe his eyes when he opened the door and saw me like that. I was dirty and unspeakably disgusting, with blackened eyes making two deep slits in my swollen face, not counting the gag-inducing smell that I was giving off. Blackie got me quickly to the bathroom where he stripped me of my soiled clothes, stuffed them into a garbage bag and ran a hot bath full of soap and an added cup of javel water to really clean me up and sterilize my cuts. Miraculously, I didn't seem to have broken anything except perhaps my nose, which had bled a lot.

An hour later, dressed in clothes that Blackie had lent me, we left in search of my aggressors, with the intention of really paying those cowards back for the beating that they had given me. Blackie lent me a jack-knife, which I had hidden in my underwear while he was carrying a fully loaded thirty-eight revolver! I have no idea what would have happened if we had actually been able to find those guys, but now I thank God for our having avoided such a massacre. (Otherwise I would be writing this book behind bars.) After checking out ten or more taverns, we gave up looking and went back to Blackie's place where he offered to put me up for the night and repaid me some of the money that I had lent him when he came out of prison.

But it was still too early to adjourn and my thirst for adventure was not yet satisfied, no more than my sick craving

*Montréal's lower town on Saint-Laurent Boulevard South

for alcohol. I left Blackie's place and headed for the "Main"*
to go and impress the patrons at the French Casino, the
Canasta and the Main Café. I became a Royal Canadian
Mounted Police officer to provide myself with all the im-
portance that my pride still needed. I had a dozen postcards
in my shirt pocket depicting a Mountie in his full-dress red
tunic that looked exactly like me. I would show this picture
of my "identical twin" to anyone who didn't believe me.
The resemblance was so striking that I almost believed it
myself. But was this a good place to identify myself as a cop,
while surrounded by petty thieves, pimps, fences, drug
dealers, and others of the same breed? Of course, not!

One could say that I was looking for new ways to get
myself killed, original means of self-destruction, cynical
plans to hasten the end to my agony. I was no longer lucid,
and my craziness made me a laughing stock. Imagine the
scene: a supposed RCMP officer, seated at a table with
criminals, bragging about his imaginary captures of bad
guys while flashing a fake badge! I was again laying myself
open to heavy retribution, but this time I avoided all that
because nobody believed me and most of them sneered at
me or broke into tears of laughter.

I finished an all-nighter at the Saint-John Café, one of
the most infamous clubs on the Main. I managed to insult
so many of the bar's patrons that I was kicked out ten minutes later. I found myself on the street, lost, dazed, and
barely able to stand. I made my way to the slums to find
refuge for the night. The next morning, in the communal
washroom of my fifty-cent-a-night shelter, I saw myself in
the mirror. I could hardly believe that that emaciated face,
dirty and scarred, was really that of André of old, fierce
competitor, number one in everything, the champ even!
The more I looked around me, the more I saw myself in the
other lost souls who had been pulled in around me, who
were a reflected picture of my own state of ruin.

This horrific image tormented a mind already undermined by remorse, and I was seized by fear and anguish. How had I managed to end up like this? Could it be because I drink too much? I began to ask myself the question without wanting an honest answer; but everything around me was unanimous, everything is silently shouting at me: "Yes, André, your problem is your alcohol consumption!"

But I was unable to admit it. I took refuge in self-pity and revulsion, realizing that I could see no way out, no means of removing this thirst without a miracle. But I didn't believe in miracles. I didn't believe in anything.

One fine sunny Friday in mid-June 1964, I was sitting on the curb in front of the Milano Tavern. It was almost ten, and I had no more money for booze and nothing to smoke. For the last ten minutes, I had had my eye on a cigarette butt lying in the gutter, but I didn't dare pick it up for fear that someone going by might see me! And still, the strength of my pride would always show itself in spite of the fact that I had become a stray, a loser, a piece of society's garbage.

I was so concentrated on the cigarette butt that I failed to notice a large vehicle had stopped right beside me and that a man had gotten out and was standing next to me: "Hello, André, what are you doing here? My God, you're in bad shape! Come inside the tavern, I want to talk to you."

It was Philippe, my childhood friend, whom my mother had asked to come and find me. Having learned of my distress and despair, she had sent one of my best friends to try to convince me to get some help. To gain my confidence, Philippe bought me a large "Brading's" beer and gave me a pack of cigarettes. Seeing my sorry state and the uncontrollable shaking in my hands, he looked at me with an air of both sadness and disbelief and said to me: "But, André, have you seen yourself in a mirror lately? It doesn't make any sense. I can barely recognize the brilliant guy I had for a friend not so long ago. Listen to me carefully because I have a proposition for you. If you agree to take the cure at the Domrémy Clinic, your parents are ready to take you back, and for my part, I promise to find you a job as soon as possible."

Did I have a choice? I was in such a weakened and humiliated state that I would agree to anything to get out of the black hole that I was in. I would even lie and promise not to take a single drink. I would have sold my soul to the devil for just one day without thirst.

"Philippe, I accept your offer, but I want to be certain that it's true that my father will let me come back home without making a big deal about it. I want to call my mother to make sure."

On the telephone my mother reassured me and seemed very happy that I had finally agreed to get some help. I gulped down what I believed to be my last beer, and we left the Milano Tavern and went to my parents' place in Outremont. I walked in the door shaking with fear and hiding behind Philippe, but the welcome was friendly and I quickly became reassured.

I spent some time with my mother in the den while my father read the paper in the living room. I could tell that he didn't believe this was going to work but that my mother had once again convinced him to help me out. There was no pity in my mother's eyes, but rather sympathy and softness, like a light of hope. Would I disappoint her again or would I finally have the necessary courage to attack my problem? I was mixed up, confused, very depressed, and I had a soul filled with anguish at the simple thought of being forced to stop drinking.

I tried to eat something, but I had no appetite. My mother packed my suitcase for the next morning when I would leave for my three-week stay at the clinic. She was careful to pack everything that I would need, including an envelope with fifty dollars of spending money in it. I spent an agitated night, my sleep interspersed with nightmares and frequent awakenings.

The following morning my brother Pierre and my friend Philippe came to take me to the Domrémy Clinic on Decarie Boulevard in Ville Saint-Laurent. We went into the admitting room where a nurse began writing up my file. Their presence no longer required, my companions left me with the nurse and departed. Since I didn't really intend to stop drinking, I stated to the nurse: "Miss, I would really like to sign in today, but I have a few important things to take care of before I take my cure. Let's fill out the forms now, and I'll be back on Monday morning for my admission to the clinic."

Her answer was clear: "My dear sir," she said, "we don't keep people here against their will, and you may come back whenever it suits you."

I rushed to sign the last of the required forms and quickly left the clinic with my suitcase while promising to return on Monday morning. I felt really good, and freed from having to go into "detox."* I made my way to the Texas Tavern close by and made new plans for the weekend. It was ten o'clock on Saturday morning. I was dying for a drink and firmly resolved to go on, what was theoretically, my last bender. To begin with, I had almost fifty dollars on me that my mother had given me. After that, I sold everything that I had, suitcase included, which gave me an additional forty dollars. And finally, I always had my trusty check book, which would save me every time!

By noon I had already filled up on about twenty glasses of beer and was off. At a brisk pace, I walked over to Dagwood's Restaurant for a steak dinner followed by a Cointreau, a beer chaser, and paid, obviously with a rubber check for fifty dollars. My bill was only for twenty, so I had another thirty to add to the hundred that I already had. I was rich again. I was on a roll! After that I went to the Val Royal station where I took the two o'clock train

*Detoxification clinic

to Saint-Placide, one of my favorite watering holes where I could get away from it all.

Between Saturday afternoon and Sunday night of this "lost weekend," I have no detailed memory of where I went. But I remember having left my base of operations, the Hotel Coin Beau Lac in Saint-Placide to go to drink in Saint-André d'Argenteuil, Grenville, and Lachute where, unconsciously, I was still trying to get back together with Claudette. My tour ended at the Hotel Chevrier, where I woke up on Sunday morning totally lost, sick as a mongrel dog, and relieved of almost all my money. I only had twenty dollars left.

I went back to Saint-Placide and drank all afternoon, coming to the end of all the money that I had left. The hotel manager gave me credit, which allowed me to keep drinking until midnight when the bar closed. Forced to leave the hotel, I was on the street with neither money nor a place to spend the night. As it was summer, I decided to sleep under the stars. I went to the public wharf that extended out into Lac des Deux-Montagnes, and I stretched out on a ramp next to the water in order to go to sleep. Full of booze, I soon fell asleep or blacked out..Then about four in the morning, the storm broke. I curled myself into a ball and for better or worse tried to protect myself from the wind and torrential rain that was washing over me. Suddenly there was a lightning strike in the water close to where I was sheltering. I panicked completely, ran like a crazy man as fast as my legs could carry me and hid under the hotel balcony.

To this day I continue to have a great fear of lightning, and whenever a storm appears on the horizon, I become worried and anxious.

Totally soaked and shivering, I spent the night in my lair like a hunted animal, overcome by anguish and my usual fears. At dawn the rain stopped, and the sun came out. It blinded me and brought out the woeful condition that I was in: worn and dirty clothes, unkempt, unshaved, eyes swollen and bloodshot to the lashes, all complemented by my morning shakes in all of my extremities caused by a gradual lack of alcohol in my system.

Was I sick! Oh, God, I wanted to die and disappear forever into nothingness. I didn't know what to do anymore and, sitting on the roadside, stunned, I awaited my fate. It was around seven in the morning, and the people who had spent the weekend in Saint-Placide were taking to the road and returning to work on a fine Monday morning in June. All of a sudden, two cars stopped in front of me. My brother and my friend Philippe, who had left me at the clinic on Saturday were shocked to find me there.

"What are you doing here? Didn't you stay at the clinic? God! Look at you! Come on, get in the car so I can take you the hell back to Domrémy!"

My brother took responsibility for driving me to the clinic, and this time he made sure that I was really taken in hand before he left. A nurse gave me a "hot" injection, and I felt myself drift off into complete unconsciousness. It was the beginning of my detoxification cure, which would last twenty-one days. That shot made me sleep for thirty-six hours straight, and when I awoke, the doctor outlined for me the treatment that I would undergo in the course of the next three weeks: medication, special diet, interviews with the psychiatrist and conversations with the chaplain if I so desired.

After a few days, I was weaned, my shakes had gone, my nightmares were not as long and were less frequent. I regained my appetite, and the medication was slowly making me feel better.

Among the forty "boarders" registered at the clinic, most were in their thirties and comprised an interesting group from various backgrounds. And when I suggested forming two fastball teams to provide us with afternoon entertainment, I had no trouble in finding the twenty players needed. The first team was called "The Pills" and the second "The Shots." With the clinic being located in a former school, we could play our games in a large asphalt-covered yard.

As the main organizer of this activity, I decided almost everything. I was in the starring role as usual. As the pitcher, I wanted to win any way I could and would often aim at the batters' heads, as I boasted about my high strike-out rate. The medication that I was prescribed obviously had no effect on my sick pride. Anyway, affected by all the drugs, the players often hurt themselves on the asphalt surface, and the male nurse never finished treating the bruises and bandaging the scrapes. He let me know that he had had enough of my brilliant ideas and that he would be asking the administration to prohibit these games.

Two days later the equipment was taken away, and the ball games were over for good.

During my stay I had to attend meetings where psychologists, doctors and psychiatrists tried to explain the real nature of our sickness to us and the ways to overcome it. I learned that I suffered from a physical allergy to alcohol that let loose an uncontrollable need to drink whenever I downed the first glass. In addition, this physical allergy is accompanied by a mental obsession, thus creating a vicious circle that locks away all feelings or all efforts to resist this unholy pair. This two-headed monster is invincible if one has not the honesty to admit that it controls one. This is the first step to take to begin a real recovery. I was also told that my sickness was incurable, but it could be sufficiently controlled to allow one to lead a nearly normal life without alcohol. I was not very surprised to also learn that it was an emotional sickness and that hypersensitivity is one of its undeniable characteristics.

Then one Thursday evening we were invited to attend a talk given by several members of Alcoholics Anonymous. Of course I had already heard about this association, and I was always puzzled by the mystery surrounding this organization. At last I could find out what it held for me, and I decided to go to the meeting. It came as an unexpected surprise, seeing these people well dressed, in shirts and ties, calm and serene, coming to tell us about their lives as active alcoholics and their recoveries thanks to the AA program. One of them told a story of his life that was so similar to my own that I was convinced that he had access to my file at the clinic.

After the meeting I went and asked him if it was really true that he had drunk so much and how was it that he no longer had to take a drink.

"I started with one twenty-four-hour period," he told me. "Then a second and a third during which other members helped me understand the steps that I had to take to succeed in controlling my sickness and, as you see, I am fine now and I have been sober for three years. You know, André, here you get treatment to recover your physical health, and you have been given theoretical explanations of your sickness, but if you want to stay sober when you leave here, you have to join our group to seriously undertake a real rehabilitation program. Otherwise you will inevitably slip and start drinking again."

Then he shook my hand, gave me his telephone number, and left me by saying: "Call me, it doesn't cost anything. I'll take you to meet my group of friends, and you can decide yourself to join us or not. There's no obligation, no membership fees. I hope to see you soon."

After the meeting we chatted with these marvelous beings who seemed to have come from another world and whom we knew to be sincere because they could not have feigned their real suffering nor their real serenity. A kind of hope was reborn in the depths of my being, and I felt that I would sleep better because perhaps there was a solution to my problem. My addiction would possibly be conquered. Yes, when I leave here, I will go and see Alcoholics Anonymous. I will try to do as they say, one day at a time, just one day at a time. This seemed to be the key that would open the door to a lasting sobriety.

At the end of the prescribed twenty-one days, I came out of my cure with renewed strength and optimism, further encouraged to undertake a new life without alcohol. My friend Philippe picked me up at the clinic and took me home to my parents, who had agreed to let me live with them again because I had stopped drinking. In my heart of hearts, I began thinking that I could do a better job of controlling my drinking and thus put my life back on an even keel. This cure that had been forced upon me would perhaps help me to find new tricks or new ways of drinking to avoid falling back into the same pattern of behavior that I had been in before. But I soon realized that my way of thinking was mistaken, and that as far as sobriety was concerned, there was no easy way for those who were affected by this insidious sickness.

That Tuesday in June of 1964, the day I left Domrémy, coincided with the Côte-des-Neiges AA group meeting, which was a short distance from my parents' place. I came on foot, and upon entering the smoky room, I came face to face with an old drinking buddy, Jean B., who broke out laughing:

"At least now that I meet you here, I know I'm in the right place! Is this your first meeting too?"

"Yeah, It's my first time, and I hope that it will lead to something soon."

Jean recounted his recent disasters with alcohol, and I did the same. It was comforting for me to know that I wasn't the only one with this damn problem. Other members of the group came to welcome me. Most of them seemed very happy to be there, and I immediately sensed a feeling of warm fellowship around me. Here there were feelings of serenity and happiness! Then the meeting started, and the person in charge explained what one had to do to become a member of Alcoholics Anonymous. One of the members read out the twelve steps needed to reach sobriety, and another person read the twelve traditions to follow in the different AA groups.

What struck me the most was the use of the word "God," which was pronounced profusely. Were the AA members practicing a religion or the founders of a new sect? In my mind, still closed and sick, I avoided like the plague any solution that included a still-vengeful God, and I greatly mistrusted anything that appeared religious, no matter what it was.

I decided to stay in the meeting right to the end anyway, which gave me the chance to hear another member tell the story of his life with alcohol and his recovery with the help of Alcoholics Anonymous. Once again, this man claimed to have had a "spiritual awakening" that enabled him to rebuild all his lives. Yeah! It felt a bit like false religiosity, and I already wondered if I was really in the right place to get some help. After the meeting, coffee was served, and several members came up to me and encouraged me to come back and to go to many other meetings if I really wanted to succeed. Jean seemed happy with his experience, and he introduced me to Jacques, who was one of the founders of the Côte-des-Neiges group and who had stayed sober for the last five years.

After a few weeks of intensive participation in various meetings across Montréal, I asked Jacques to be my "sponsor" to guide me in my recovery.

The reason why I chose him was that he was a bit atheistic, a little less likely to use the word "God." Rather he spoke of a "Higher" or "Cosmic Power." He had a relatively simple philosophy, and his two sayings were: "Slow and easy does it" and "One day at a time." There was nothing about praying, nothing about spirituality . . . it was simple . . . just let yourself be carried by the AA movement, and its members, and sobriety will come.

From the first week of my abstinence, I went looking for a job, and I sent out innumerable curriculum vitaes. I didn't even get one interview, and none of my efforts bore any fruit. The weeks passed slowly, and I soon made it to the two months of abstinence level without too much effort. It was so easy that I began asking myself if I really was an alcoholic after all. I was not really in a very positive frame of mind after I came out of treatment at Domrémy and doubt, confusion, and even my inability to honestly admit that I was powerless in the face of alcohol (the first step in the program), prevented me from progressing toward the serenity that AA promised. I again became aggressive toward everyone, especially in relation to Jacques, my sponsor, who never stopped repeating that time would fix things, that I should accept my condition, and that I would soon be presented with my three-month medallion of sobriety in the AA. Three months already! Unbelievable but true. . . .

But I was still ashamed to admit that I was powerless in the face of alcohol, and I wasn't about to make a spectacle of myself in front of the whole AA group by taking that damned medallion and thanking God. That demanded the sort of humility that I simply didn't have. Once again, Jacques delivered his "Slow and easy does it." That was all it took to make me lose my patience, and I mouthed off at him: "That sure is a nice saying. It's easy for you to give to others when you're so well fixed yourself. You have a job, a nice car, your wife and kids, money in your pocket, what else? As for me, I've been looking for a job for almost three months. I'm still living off my parents. I don't have a woman in my life. I have to walk, and I don't have a cent. I'm fed up with your 'slow and easy does it'!"

In my wild imagination I thought that the AA was providing a black list to employers that prevented members with less than a year of sobriety from being hired. I was obviously still sick and was suffering from chronic paranoia, which made me distrust even those who were ready to do everything to help me. But my mind was closed to all their suggestions, and my predictable relapse was coming very soon.

One night Jacques said to me: "André, you complain about not being able to find a job after two months of sobriety. For the last fifteen years, you have destroyed everything in your path, and now you expect everything to return to normal in only two months? Does this make sense to you? So stop feeling sorry for yourself. Think about all those people who are still on the street and have nothing in spite of their abstinence. At least you have a roof over your head, fine parents, and new friends in AA. You're not taking the time to let time do its job. Come on, stop complaining!"

Since my desire to drink again was returning, my obsession wouldn't let me be until the day my sick mind was convinced that I wasn't an alcoholic because I was able to stop any time. It was the AA people who were preventing me from getting a job (I thought to myself), and I should quit this movement before it was too late. Now that I was convinced that I could control my consumption and drink reasonably, I could no longer see any problem with leading a normal life and returning to the "real" world of ordinary people. A few days before reaching my third month of sobriety, I planned my escape from my parents to recover my lost freedom. Without any self-doubt, since I was now certain that I had some measure of control over my drinking, I made my way to the unholy abyss of my slavery, toward suffering and the gradual death of all of my remaining hopes.

I was now so thirsty that nothing could stop me from falling back into alcohol again. It was the Labor Day weekend, September 1964, and my parents were leaving for Saint-Placide to close up the summer cottage. It was a dream opportunity for me to disappear, to escape the prison of my abstinence, and to make my getaway. I excused myself from going with them by saying I had to attend some AA meetings, I was champing at the bit to take my first drink. As soon as they left, I packed my bag while having an Old Paar scotch on the rocks. I searched the drawers and came up with about three hundred dollars hidden here and there.

Knowing full well that I couldn't get far with that amount, I decided to take some easily sold items with me. Downing more glasses of scotch to give me courage and deaden my guilt, I took a box and stuffed it with everything that I could: the finest bottles from my father's liquor cabinet, some of my mother's jewelry, a .32-caliber revolver, and some other things that I could unload to the tavern buyers. I called a taxi, took all my loot with me, and, as a bonus, I lifted my father's brand new TV!

"Driver, to the Rockland Tavern please."

Once I had gotten out of the cab with all my gear, I sold the TV to the tavern manager for a hundred dollars, and I liquidated the rest of my "merchandise" for about one hundred and fifty. It was only five o'clock, and I was already fairly tipsy.

I had to find a room to rent as soon as possible, and I instinctively ended up at my most recent haunt, the Milano Tavern where I took up again with my old drinking buddies. There was a rooming house above the tavern, and its owner was a faithful patron of the Milano. He had only one room available, and it was on the third floor. He offered it to me for eight dollars a week if I would pay him a month in advance. Keys in hand, I climbed up to my new nest and quickly moved in. Back down to the tavern, I bought a round of beer for everyone to the great satisfaction of all my "friends." I asked if there was any work in the neighborhood, if there were still circulars to deliver, or if there were any other openings. Then eleven o'clock came, and it was the last call before closing. I downed my last beers and went up to my room with the painful knowledge that I had again fallen into the same pattern that I was in before my forced cure.

A very strong feeling of guilt swept over me, and I threw myself sobbing onto my bed while knowing that by leaving AA, I had gone and sabotaged my only chance to end my problems. The mirror on my dresser reflected an image of a lost André, deeply unhappy and without hope. How had I been able to fail once more? Why was this desire to drink so overwhelming? The turbulence of my thoughts continually led me back into the sorrow of having stolen from my parents and of having lied to myself by making myself believe that I could control my drinking. I went to sleep in the confusing fog of regret, lost in the dark world of my old nightmares.

I awoke with a start at noon, and the horror of what I had done the day before overwhelmed me; what a vile rat I was! A thief and a liar, incapable of any honesty toward myself or toward all the others who had tried to help me. When would I be ready to admit my wrongs, be able to stand before the infernal bottle that was destroying all my lives, and to say that I had had enough? I really thought that I had missed my last chance, and I told myself that it was better to end it as quickly as possible by letting myself drift surely toward a release that only death could bring. Having destroyed my spiritual life and lost my faith, I sabotaged my emotional life by destroying my only true love, Claudette, and rejecting the love of my parents. I also ruined my professional life. I only had a small semblance of a physical life left, with my health tottering on the brink and a shadow of a mental life undermined by a mass of unhealthy and uncontrollable emotions. On this fine sunny Sunday, I could see the end to my torment approaching. I had nothing else to lose. My human dignity had been stripped away and was already lost among the ruins of my wasted talent. The only thing left for me to do was to drink until the last agonizing periods of consciousness were over.

My remaining cash would certainly not be enough to slake this burning thirst, which was eating me up, and I began to think of ways of improving my situation. In light of my "professional standing," it would be difficult if not impossible to find interesting work no matter what it was. I had to be content with a little of what was available and be ready to con or steal if that wasn't enough. At the point I was at, I had no more conscience. I was totally unaccountable for my actions. I would probably have gone as far as killing someone for a few drinks. The only thing I wouldn't do was to beg on street corners like some of my "associates" did. Neither did I ask for welfare, being too proud to lower myself to live off others. I wanted nothing from this rotten society. I wanted to conserve my false freedom to choose my lot by myself, even if it killed me!

I don't intend to repeat the chapter "The Point of No Return" here, since I had returned to the same stage I was at before I encountered Alcoholics Anonymous. My physical health had improved little by little, but mentally and psychologically my sickness continued to progress in such a way that my relapse into drinking would lead me to new depths that were worse than my preceding trials (if such things were possible). But it was worse than before since I now knew that a solution existed, but I had rejected it because I was too proud and dishonest. This last life line was the AA program, which I had stayed away from for no reason more viable than my alcoholic madness. I denied the only remedy for my problems outside of immediate or gradual suicide.

In such a despairing state of mind, the sick and nearly insane person that I had become could not do otherwise than to seek out his ultimate destruction. The emotional suffering, the deep sickness of the soul became a habit for me. Remorse was eating me alive, and I became totally obsessed with deep feelings of guilt regarding my parents,

Claudette, my friends, and everyone else, I had treated like dirt. I had to drink as fast as I could to try to forget all those painful memories.

My money wasn't going to last more than a few days longer, and I had to find ways to get rich again fairly soon. I had been well known for a long time at the Milano Tavern, so as soon as it opened on Monday morning, I went up to the bartender manager to ask him to give me the tavern-cleaning "contract." The only job available consisted of taking out the garbage cans in the morning. The pay for this work was at the rate of ten glasses of beer or a dollar a day. At least my morning eye-opener was guaranteed, and I became the tavern's "sanitation worker." Around nine o'clock, the circular-distribution boss made his appearance in the tavern, looking for some "flyer guys": "Hi there, Ti-Paul. Remember me? I've done the job for you before." "Yeah, and I also remember that the inspector fired you." I reassured him by telling him that I was in better shape than before and I now had a handle on my drinking.

"I'm going to give you another chance at a dollar an hour, but if you screw up again, you won't last long; you can start today, the truck leaves in ten minutes."

And just like that, I again became the eminent circular distributor, one first step to vagrancy. To put me in training, Ti-Paul gave me Christophe-Colomb and Saint-Denis, nicknamed "Ladder Streets," because of all the stairways found there. But Domrémy and AA had gotten me back in shape, and on the first day, I was in fighting form, carried by my morning drinking and the freedom that I had just recovered. However, three weeks later, I was back to where I was just before I was forced to go to Domrémy, without a cent, unable to pay my room rent because I was drinking away everything as soon as I earned it. Physically weakened again, I lost my job as a circular distributor and was reduced to picking night-crawlers for a bait company. I spent the night on the golf courses in Sainte-

Therese where we had to endure rain or lawn sprinklers while picking worms with both hands as long as our poor backs could take it.

You had to see us: poor weak slobs, miner's lamps strapped to our foreheads, boxes tied to our waists to dump our worms into whenever our cans were full. Cans were attached to our right legs with tape while other cans full of sawdust were stuck to our left legs to wipe our fingers with, whenever they became too slimy and slippery to catch more worms. At dawn the truck would take us back to Montréal to the Pére Gédéon Tavern for a breakfast, which consisted of a hard-boiled egg and ten glasses of beer, all for a dollar, the "daily special" right! Picking an average of two thousand worms between ten in the evening and six in the morning, I earned about ten dollars for my night's work. After breakfast, I returned to the Milano to begin my day job by carrying out the garbage for another dollar, another ten glasses of draft beer. What a fine day lay ahead of me, what a promising future I had!

My poor carcass couldn't endure that sort of punishment for long, and I had to give up worm hunting because of my lack of productivity. The last night I had to stop after only an hour.

My legs cramped up, overcome by dizziness, soaked to the skin, frozen to the bone, I had to wait under a tree until morning when I was put into the truck amidst the laughter and sarcasm of my coworkers. My serious physical affliction had begun. My shakes were becoming more frequent and more violent than before, and my only recourse left was the Milano Tavern where I was endured and tolerated due to the lack of better patrons. I hung out with the petty criminals in hopes of discovering a few other tricks to get my hands on some easy money. I was starting to fear the winter which would soon be here, bringing cold and misery to the "Homeless" club of which I was a full member. My vagrancy was progressing, I no longer had a permanent address. When night came I made my way from one doorway to another, one heat grate to another. I went to all-night restaurants, and at dawn the cycle began again at my "Milano Castle."

Some circular distributors lifted checks from mail boxes and asked me if I could find a way to cash them. It was the beginning of my career as a minor fraud artist. The new unexpected "job" provided me with a new source of income, enabling me to drink and buy rounds for my accomplices, who kept fifty percent of the take for themselves. But no matter how much I earned, I never had enough to pay rent, although from time to time I would stay at a-dollar-a-night flop house and I could afford a breakfast or two every week.

Almost all my money went into alcohol and occasionally for a glass of oysters with strong cheese accompanied by adulterated alcohol. I didn't know that if I got caught at this little con game, I risked going to jail for a couple of years. But I no longer had any conscience. The holy bottle, on becoming my full-time mistress, left no room for my disappearing reason. I cashed these stolen checks at local businesses and even dared to try a few banks. With this extra money I was able to visit other taverns and clubs like the Lion d'Or, the Champs de Lys, the Hotel Lafayette, all notorious and well-known hangouts of small-time crooks. During this whole time, I never had a woman. I was convinced that being so dirty, even a prostitute wouldn't take my money. At any rate I was so run down and physically weak that any sexual performance was probably beyond me.

There were weeks when the checks were few and far between, and to make it to the end of the month, I had to resort to other strategies. One of the tavern regulars introduced me to sign language for the hearing impaired and invited me to go around with him while he handed out sign-language cards and begged for a bit of money. I practiced this "profession" for a few weeks, which allowed me to survive until the next round of stolen checks arrived. But one night I decided to hand out my cards to private homes and apartments. I had the misfortune of knocking on the door of a real deaf person. He made a string of signs that I couldn't recognize, and I could see in his eyes that he knew he was on to me and was dealing with an impostor. I fled as fast as I could, knowing full well that real deaf people would not be amused to find someone stealing their means of livelihood. A few days later, I heard tell that the guy who taught me this trick had ended up with both legs broken.

Returning to my habitual activities, I was approached by a suspicious-looking guy who wanted to sell me a check-writing machine and even a few commercial check books recently stolen from a business in the north of town. I told him that I had no money at the moment, but it wouldn't be long before the income tax rebate checks were mailed.

"Don't bother with that," he said. "I also have a series of travelers' checks that you could redeem, and you can pay me with the cash from a few of those."

I jumped at the opportunity, and a little while later, a local plumber who always had pockets full of money sat down at my table and asked if I could do him a small favor. He showed me a construction contract and knowing that I had already worked in that field, he asked me to advise him on the validity of different clauses. To thank me he bought me twenty glasses of beer.

I quickly went through the contract in question and advised him on all the legal aspects while suggesting several clarifications or minor changes. Taking advantage of his good mood, I took my turn in asking him for a small service: "Could you cash a traveler's check for me? I need some money right away, but the bank's closed."

Even if I intimated that the check's origin was questionable, he agreed to give me fifty dollars.

"With all the checks I deposit, it will go through unnoticed. Don't worry about that, I'll arrange everything."

I now had enough money to go and rent a room on Wolfe Street south of Saint-Catherine where a number of my street friends stayed. I went right away, the check-writing machine under one arm and my green garbage bag full of all the old clothes I had left under the other. I was so excited, that I was practically running!

The owners of this rooming house were two elderly spinsters who seemed quite naive and withdrawn. I offered to pay four weeks rent at eight dollars a week and gave them a one hundred dollar travelers' check, which they took right away while returning my sixty-six dollars change. I surely was becoming richer by the minute, and I went upstairs to move in to my new quarters.

I put my machine on the only table in the room and emptied the garbage bag onto the bed. In it were some dirty clothes, an envelope containing forged papers, my unemployment insurance book, and photos of the construction sites in Labrador where I had worked in the past. It was nothing to write home about. I threw my rags into the garbage can, and I decided to renew my "wardrobe" with the little money I had. I went to Rossy's Department Store on Ontario Street and for thirty dollars. I bought underwear, socks, shirts, one pair of pants, etc.

When I returned to Wolfe Street, my landladies asked me to tea so they could get to "know me better." I was happy to accept, and led them to believe that I could "read" the tea leaves and foresee the future. I sensed that they were very superstitious, and I saw a way to have some fun at their expense while conning them out of more money with other travelers' checks that they cashed without raising an eyebrow.

During the months following, I was ripping people off left, right, and center, while always suspecting that the police had their eye on me and were waiting to catch me in the act. One day while I was busy getting drunk at the Milano, I learned that my plumber friend had been arrested in a stolen-check case. I was certain to be implicated because he was one of my preferred outlets. The week after, his wife came to the tavern and begged me to go to court to testify on her husband's behalf to get him out of this mess. She gave me a guarantee that I was in no danger of being arrested for complicity. I agreed to meet with the plumber's lawyer, who assured me that I could testify under legal immunity. So I went down to the court house to testify that it really was I who had given him the checks and that he had no idea that they had been stolen. The judge immediately released him, and I was roundly applauded when I returned to the tavern with my exonerated friend.

I knew that the police were now watching me and that my room to maneuver was shrinking from day to day. That didn't stop me from using my check-writing machine to produce my "paycheck" every Friday. I exchanged these forged bank drafts at one restaurant or another, one club or another, at businesses, and even in certain banks. My little racket lasted for a few more weeks until the day that I found out at the tavern that the police had traced the stolen travelers' checks back to the Wolfe Street rooming house where I was still living. I hurried to get my stuff out of there, to destroy the forged company checks and to throw the machine down the sewer in the alley behind the house. Before leaving I warned the landladies that I would put a curse on them if they ever went to the police over the travelers' checks that they had accepted. I later learned, being so superstitious, they never dared to.

I succeeded in making it through the winter of 1965. I survived the cold, the hunger, and all the other miseries that I haven't described here. My only comfort was alcohol, no matter where it came from, and I felt myself slowly sliding down the slope of total indifference, which I mistakenly took for freedom. When spring came I went back to delivering circulars and eking out my daily existence in an increasing stupor. I was only a shadow of my former self. I had lost at least twenty-five pounds. I was covered with scars and bruises caused by numerous falls as well as the blows I had received. I dared not touch any stolen checks because I felt that the police had me under surveillance and were following me. I was filled with fear and new agonies, and the relief that came from drinking waned since the effect of alcohol was no longer what it was.

I had become so dirty and unsightly that a grocery store owner (one of the large chains) prohibited me from entering his store: "I don't want to see you in my store. Take your circulars and leave, and when you come back to get paid, wait for me outside because you're scaring off my customers!" I really felt like taking this businessman by the throat and throttling him to death, but I had neither the courage nor the strength and, like a beaten dog with its tail between its legs, I went back to the Milano, cursing God for allowing me to undergo such humiliation.

I had come to the point where nothing could stop me from drinking even if alcohol was no longer effective in totally deadening my guilt and remorse. Almost all the ways for me to find money looked good, and I was always on the lookout for any occasion that would put some cash into my hands. Autumn came with its chills, rain and sadness. I felt that I couldn't get through another winter, that I hadn't the strength, that my thirst would be extinguished when I was. I was constantly grinding out darkness while looking for an escape, a final solution to this non-life that I was unable to endure much longer.

Then one morning in October, I met three thieves who suggested that I join them for some small burglaries in private homes. Like I said, I was not averse to anything, so I went along. Together we consulted the obituary columns in the papers, wanting to take advantage of the families of the deceased, who were absent from their homes while at the funeral parlor or the cemetery. It was the easiest kind of house breaking! Words like dirty, low-down, and rotten are too nice a description for such behavior. With a skinful to calm my nerves, I left in the truck with these villains to participate in my first break-and-enter.

All the usual precautions were taken by my skilled associates in this profession. They broke a single pane of glass in the door, and we broke into this third-story apartment. My accomplices quickly rifled through all the drawers to find money and jewelry. They seemed to know all the hiding places. As for me, I didn't know what to take. I was clumsy because of my inexperience and to top it off, I was too drunk to act in a quick and efficient manner. Suddenly we heard the sound of a car in front of the house and my companions left in a hurry while urging: "Come on, André, let's get out of here fast!" But I couldn't go fast and I took the time to slip on a woman's fur coat over my jacket, put two liquor bottles that I had found on the sideboard into my bag, and grab a portable radio and carry it under my arm.

I ran out the back door into the lane to catch up to my accomplices, but they had already taken the truck and driven off. There I was with my loot in the pouring rain, like a scene from a movie comedy! But it was far from funny. I had to make a quick getaway from the scene of the crime. I ran like a man possessed and was able jump (miraculously) onto a waiting bus to the great amusement of the other passengers, who asked me if I wasn't celebrating Halloween a bit early! The trip to lower town completed, I entered the tavern with my booty to share it with my companions, who seemed very surprised to see me, thinking that I had been caught by the police. They immediately led me outside to the alley to hide the stolen property in a large empty garbage bin. Coming back inside they gave me fifty dollars for everything (minus a bottle of scotch that I had secretly hidden from them). They told me to disappear from the neighborhood for a few days, fearing that I would only raise suspicions with my behavior as an amateur break-in artist. I had just lost another "job"; I could not even make a good thief.

That night I stayed at the Meurling shelter after having shared my scotch with the other rubbies from Viger Square on Craig Street.* I had seven or eight new friends with whom I could drink the alcohol that we had found, bought, or occasionally stolen. We had become experts in the making of "cocktails" each one tastier than the next, using scotch, rye, or gin mixed with rubbing alcohol, shaving lotion, perfume, melted shoe polish and whatever else as ingredients. We drank this dynamite mix, which insured an almost instantaneous high, protecting us from heat or cold and shutting us off from the world around us. It was comforting to know that these friends could always provide me with my "daily medicine" since I too took my turn furnishing such elixirs as I found here and there.

It was fully autumn, and at the beginning of November, I was overcome with anguish, feeling the cold, and my everyday insecurities added to my fears. I had to drink greater and greater quantities of alcohol, stronger and stronger poisons, to calm myself, to stop the convulsions, to diminish the frequency of my nightmares that sometimes got me expelled from the shelters where I had taken refuge for the night. My dreams became delirium tremens where pictures of horror multiplied within my sick mind, where the rats gnawing at my feet became bigger and bigger, more voracious, more hideous. It was Hell on earth. Day by day my suffering was becoming more unbearable. However, my thirst remained. My madness lived off it and drove me to hang onto the remnants of a life that I continued to destroy.

*Equivalent to "The Bowery" in New York City.

One Saturday some Black American tourists came into the tavern to ask for information about places to visit in Montréal. Right away I offered to be their tour guide, and there I was, driving off in their fancy car with them on a road to "nowhere" that they would not soon forget. I drove the two American couples to the Université de Montréal, Saint-Joseph's Oratory, and other such places. Following that, I suggested we go and see Dorval Airport before returning downtown. They agreed, seeming satisfied with my choices and the tour I had organized. When we got to the airport, I took the wrong turn by following a tanker truck that was going along beside the tarmac to refuel the planes; realizing my error, I made a U-turn, unaware that I was now driving down a landing strip! We found ourselves in international territory, an extremely dangerous no man's land.

I was chased by two Royal Canadian Mounted Police cars that signaled me to follow them off the airfield. The police escorted me up to the exit and ordered me to go to the RCMP office to be identified. Luckily, I got lost again and couldn't find their famous office. I took off along Côte-de Liesse and the Trans Canada expressway, speeding all the way. I could see the flashers of the police cars far behind me. They finally lost us in the traffic. My tourists were dying of laughter and asked to visit a downtown club or two; like me they were fairly blasted and their wish to go clubbing suited me perfectly. My adventure with the Americans ended at the Lion d'Or, an infamous club (at the time) situated at the corner of Ontario and Papineau Streets.

After a few rounds, I became more drunk and went into my aggressive phase. I stared at a gorilla who was seated at the bar just to the point at which he lost his patience and told me to get out. I provoked him by insultingly suggesting that he take a walk and offered to fight. He was twice as big as I was, but I wasn't afraid of anything. Alcohol gave me a false and mindless bravado and kept my fear in check. He came straight for me, and before I had a chance to react, he gave me a very hard shot to the nose, and I went crashing ten feet backwards taking tables and chairs with me. I was semiconscious, blood was streaming from my broken nose, and before I could get up, he began kicking me in the ribs and back. I was saved by the bartender who stopped the carnage and called an ambulance. But I refused to go to the hospital, saying that I was not seriously injured.

The tourists had fled, and I went down the street looking for somewhere to spend the night. On Papineau Street I found an abandoned triplex, and I climbed all the way up to the third floor where the only furniture was an old stove. The place was dirty and littered with all sorts of junk. I stuffed the heater with paper and bits of wood. I lit the fire and stretched out on the floor to go to sleep. I couldn't sleep without falling into my habitual nightmares, and my nose started to really bleed again. The horrors of the night passed with first light, so I hurried back to the Milano to warm up and clean my wounds in the tavern washroom. This latrine was the only place where I could still wash up a bit. I saw my swollen face in the mirror, and I jumped backwards. Was that really me? What kind of sordid creature had I become? When could I die? When would this unremitting torment end?

The weeks following were all the same in their continuing misery. My ongoing vagrancy got me mired in a lethargy of unawareness. I could almost not feel the cold or the pain in my body, destroyed on the inside by doctored alcohol and swollen on the outside by daily injuries. I rarely left my cocoon in the Milano, overcome as I was by my fear of being arrested by the police or of being recognized by one of the victims of my many frauds. One day I took a chance by leaving my seclusion, and I ventured out onto Ontario Street in search of cigarette butts, unaware that I was being followed by some unsavory characters. Opposite Delorimier Street, I was grabbed and hustled off to a deserted basement.

I recognized one of them, who said: "Aren't you the check artist? Aren't you the one who screwed everyone around here? You've finished ripping us off, you bastard, and now it's payback time for all the crooked schemes you've pulled on the people and businesses in our neighborhood!"

Without another word they shoved me up against the wall and began really working me over. I collapsed, and the kicks came hard and fast and caught me everywhere including my ribs, the small of my back, and my crotch. They left me for dead, knocked out by all those blows. Sometime later I came out of my coma, revived by a tavern regular who overheard a guy boasting about the beating that he had given me. Since I had already helped my savior out in the past by lending him some money, which, by the way, he still owed me, he felt sorry for me and offered to take me to his room and fix me up. But I couldn't stand up on my own, and I couldn't walk. My kidneys were bruised, and he had to hail a taxi. My new friend and the driver succeeded in getting me into the cab and back to his room. I had to spend four days on my back, loaded with booze and painkillers.

On the fifth day, I had enough strength and courage to hobble back to the tavern. My buddies Tonton and Ti-Cul Moisan were shocked to see me and almost didn't recognize me as I was so bashed up.

I made it through the holidays for better or worse, and my life as a vagrant didn't add up to much. I had no idea how to get off that infernal treadmill. In my sick mind, I pieced together all sorts of scenarios. I made big plans to score enough money to get me out of that hell hole of slow death. But no one would go along with me, and most of them thought I had gone totally crazy or was incapable of pulling it off no matter how good the idea was. All my long do-nothing days ended with the waiter's shout of "Last call!" And they were followed by my dark fears each night.

I made a habit of going down to Viger Square with my friend Moisan to drink a bit of "antifreeze" with the gang from the square in order to make it easier to get through the night. Around two in the morning, stoned and wasted by the cold, we would make our way to the delivery van full of advertising circulars. This was our new dorm where we slept every night. After guzzling down the last gulps from our bottles, we would cover ourselves with four or five layers of circulars to keep out the cold and damp of another goddamn winter night.at twenty-two degrees below zero, what could be better?

In the morning we would get up, totally parched, half-frozen, shaking all over because we were out of fuel. Stomachs and throats burnt by last night's poison, we would emerge from our "room" to quickly put out the fire by stuffing ourselves with snow and bits of ice. After that, we would crawl our way to the tavern where we slumped against the heaters to thaw out our frozen extremities. . . . And the daily grind would begin again, I take out the garbage cans, Tonton comes into the john, force-feeding my first beers to still the shakes, and for me, another "enchanting" day would begin.

It was January 1966, and winter's cold had come for good. Our van shelter had become our regular bedroom, and my friend Moisan continued to be my roommate. We shared the circulars that were our blankets as well as the assorted drinks that we made, but one of those mornings at the end of January, in a twenty-five below zero Siberian cold snap, Moisan didn't wake up as usual, before I did.

I shook him as hard as I could: "Hey, Moisan, get up, you'll be late for your circular deliveries."

I really shook him, hit him, shouted at him, but nothing worked. I saw that his lips were blue, his face was a stark white instead of the usual wine red that I was used to seeing. . . . Moisan was dead! I ran to the tavern to call the police, who, when they got there, could only confirm his death. I told the delivery boss that Moisan was dead and that I was ready to take his place that day.

"Forget it, André," he told me. "You can't even go up two sets of stairs in a row. I can't trust you to do it."

It seems to me that Moisan's death should have made me reflect on my own agonizing condition. But no, the only thing I found to do better was to try to take his job so I could go on living my little life and continuing to stay mired in the sludge of my existence. I had really come to the bottom of the abyss. I could do nothing more.

"Oh God! Do something, because I can't do anything. If you truly exist, get me out of this hell of mine or I will end it myself."

I said these words without much conviction, but as a grand tirade because I had great difficulty in finding enough humility to ask for help from anyone, let alone a vengeful God who had done nothing but punish me for such a long time.

5

The First Miracles

February 1966 came with the last major cold spells of winter; I now slept alone in my dormitory van, Moisan was dead. I had only one brother in misfortune left, "Crippled Tonton," who stuck to me since the others had rejected him because of his filth and bad smell. Tonton was a beggar and I was a vagrant, a pair of transients who no longer saw their own reflections in life's mirror, wallowing in a total loss of human dignity. No, I really believed that it was impossible for me to sink any lower on this earth and that I had finally reached rock bottom. Only a miracle could get me out of this. But I was not the sort who believed in miracles. I would sooner leave room for hopelessness and an utter lack of faith in whom or whatever it was.

And still, in spite of how deep the abyss I was in, regardless of the kind of nothingness that surrounded me, the smell of death that weighed on me, I had a premonition that things would soon come to a head. Perhaps my desperate appeal to this God would be answered. Would this first act of humility, this first call for help, this admission of powerlessness be beneficial? That same night, curled up beneath a six-inch thick blanket of flyers, I prayed once again to this unknown God to rescue me or put me out of my misery as he had for Moisan. For the first time in a long while, my sleep was not disturbed by the ugly rats of my nightmares, and the cold of the night didn't seem to affect me.

I awoke around seven and made my way to Milano's. It

was minus 25 degrees on this Saturday, and I was frozen to the bone and shaking violently. But I knew my "cure" was waiting for me at the tavern because, as usual, Tonton would "treat" me by dumping half a gallon of poisoned alcoholic elixir down my throat to eliminate my morning convulsions. It took an hour of such treatment to get me to the point where I could at last take on a new day. And that day was to be very special!

The week before, I had cooked up a daring scheme that would get me out of all my troubles; I set it up with some professional break-in artists to make the big score that would bring in enough money to give me a fresh start. It was a plan that I had concocted while totally under the influence. It required getting a truck into the basement garage of the chosen house in order to strip the premises from the inside. Thus hidden from the prying eyes of the neighbors, it would be easy for us to grab the best stuff without taking a lot of chances since no one was at home during the day. One of my accomplices arrived at the tavern around nine-thirty and let me know that it was impossible to "do the job" that day: "André, our van driver was arrested last night, so we have to put things off."

With that he quickly left the tavern after asking the bartender to give me six glasses of draft beer as if to make up for the inconvenience. Without ever suspecting it, the most important turn of events in my life was about to take place within the next few hours.

I remained somewhat stunned and disappointed by this setback, finding myself like this, once again robbed of a solution to my problems. So how long must I wait? I mechanically took out the house plan hidden under my shirt to destroy it in case the police searched me one of those nights while they were arresting me for vagrancy.

What follows in my narrative is hard to explain because, from this time on, mysterious events began to take place. There was unusual behavior on my part, and I was seized by odd feelings of emotion. It was now ten o'clock, being the time of day when I was the least affected by alcohol, meaning that I was almost lucid for about half an hour. It was also the time when my thirst was the strongest, as I was free from my shakes and my nausea, and I felt in good enough shape to take off again in my uncontrolled drinking. To my horror I discovered that the plan I had drawn (when I was totally drunk) was a sketch of my parents' place!

Normally I wouldn't have reacted to this situation since I had already ripped my parents off on numerous occasions in the past. But this morning I was not in my usual state. The fact of seeing the "whole" of my parents' house on the plan put me in such a state of shock and made me so emotional that I had a strong urge to burst into tears.

A mysterious force flows into me and suddenly I no longer feel alone in my decisions and actions. Mechanically and without quite realizing what I am doing, I turn the plan over, and draw a line in the center of the blank sheet, and on one side I write down everything life has given me: ability, health, good parents, good friends, good employers, good education, etc. On the other side of the line, I try to write down my accomplishments resulting from all the gifts I have been given, and I realize that there isn't anything; there's nothing worth writing down! Without being aware of it, I am in the process of undertaking the fourth step that I have been taught in AA eighteen months earlier: "a searching moral inventory of myself."

Faced with this accounting of my life, I decide that I must go back to AA and give myself one last chance; but with the horrible shape I'm in, it's impossible for me to try unless I go back to the detox clinic. All the things I am now doing surprise me. Why today? I am like an automaton responding to a reborn conscience, and I have no doubt that my last night's prayer will soon be answered. I go to the phone booth, look up the number for the Domrémy Clinic, and start dialing the call.

Someone answers immediately: "Domrémy Clinic, Duchaine here."

"Hello, Mr. Duchaine, it's André speaking. Do you remember the fastball pitcher?"

"Oh, yes. How could I forget? What can I do for you?"

"Do you have room for me? I can't stand it anymore. I've decided to stop drinking."

"You were so much trouble the last time you were in this clinic that I'm not too keen on seeing you here again, and anyway, I'm not sure if we have a place for you. Call me back later." Nevertheless, he took down my number at the tavern, and he hung up.

A bit disappointed, I went back to my table while grumbling: "Even Domrémy doesn't seem to want me!"

The six glasses were still sitting in front of me, and I tried to down one of them, but you could say that I wasn't thirsty. "I AM NOT THIRSTY!" I couldn't believe it. This was the exact time of day when my desire to drink was at its strongest. So I thought that the beer must be "skunky" with a bad taste that made it undrinkable. I tried once again by tasting another of the six glasses: same reaction. This couldn't be! I asked Tonton to try one and he downed it in a hurry because he was always thirsty. He affirmed that the beer tasted very good and that it was me who had the messed up taste buds.

All of a sudden, the public telephone began to ring; I ran to answer it, certain that it was for me.

"Hello!" I said.

"André, is that you? Duchaine here. I found you a place, but I've got to warn you that the moment you step out of line, you're out the door."

"Don't worry. This time I'll behave. When can I come?"

"There's an opening today. If you don't come now, I

112

can't guarantee you another time."

"I'll be there today."

I hung up and went back to my table.

I tried one more time to take a drink, thinking that this would be my last opportunity before I took my cure; but once again I couldn't get past the second swallow. What was happening to me? Was this real? It would be really unbelievable that my thirst would vanish so easily. Was that all it took, one act of humility on my part, a vague prayer to a God whom I didn't know anymore? I had no answer. I was in a state of total confusion. But whatever was going on, I no longer was in control of my actions. I felt myself being carried by a strange presence that was leading me toward new horizons. It was only later that I understood what had happened to me. Thus I can find no other explanation than the word "miracle," the only word that I can use for the disappearance of this uncontrollable desire to drink that had made my life a living hell for more than eighteen years. But at the time, I had no suitable clothing, I was in rags, and I didn't think I would be able to go to the clinic in such a state. I decided to call my mother to ask her to help me out.

"Hello, Mother? It's André speaking. How are you?"

"Oh! I'm fine, but what's happened to you? I haven't heard from you in months!"

"Things aren't going well. I haven't anything to wear, and I need a suitcase with clean clothes since I've decided to stop drinking and go back to Domrémy again. Could you get it ready for me and send it to me by taxi? I don't even have a bus ticket to come and get it."

"My poor dear André, this would be one suitcase too many that I've packed for you. You've sold them for drinks every time. No, if you really actually do go to Domrémy, we'll bring you what you need there. From now on, you're on your own. Good luck and take care of yourself."

I was somewhat disappointed as I went back to my

table and, for the third time, I tried to gulp down my remaining beers before going to the clinic. *IT'S NO USE, MY THIRST HAS DEFINITELY GONE!* I gave my six beers to Tonton, who was dumbfounded, and as I was going out the door, I heard him yell: "That's it, folks. André has really gone nuts this morning. He gave me all his beer, and he seems completely out of it!"

Tonton knew me well, and his reaction was no surprise because he realized that especially at that time in the morning I was ready to kill for a drink and hell would freeze before I would offer a single glass to anyone. But the miracle continued to work within me, giving me the courage and determination to get myself to the clinic. In spite of the cold and regardless of my physical weakness, I drove myself to cover a distance of almost six miles on foot. I stopped from time to time here and there in a doorway, in a store of some kind or other to warm up for a few minutes before going on my way. As incredible as it seems, I managed this tour de force, and I got to Domrémy around four o'clock in the afternoon, after walking for about five hours in the freezing cold of February. In my condition, to go from Ontario Street and make it on foot to Riviere-des-Prairies surely counts as a miracle, and I have no hesitation in saying this because I know that neither the strength nor the courage were within me to accomplish such a feat. This courage came to me from somewhere else. This mysterious courage had no other explanation than the grace of a Higher Power.

My "slip" had lasted eighteen months.

As on my first stay at the clinic, I had to undergo "hot" injections and other medications, which literally knocked me out for three days in a row. Following that came the meetings with the therapists, doctors, psychiatrists and the chaplain for those who so wished. Contrary to my last visit, I seemed to be more willing and open-minded, being less argumentative with my advisors and more ready to try to understand the deviousness and complexity of the illness of alcoholism. My arrogance as well as the fatalism that resided within me before seemed to have disappeared.

I really wondered what was happening. I no longer recognized myself. Was the mild-mannered person I had become really me? If it was me, then a sudden peace had silenced the tumult of my emotions. It was only after looking back over many months of sobriety that I finally understood what had overcome me because at the time of this total transformation of my interior, I hadn't the slightest idea what was in the process of actually happening.

In the months and years that followed, many unexplainable events took place. Previously I had attributed these mysteries to chance, happenstance, or fortuitous coincidence. But, as my years of sobriety mounted up, I regained my faith in a Higher Power that had intervened in my life on that morning when my strong desire to drink disappeared never to return. Starting from that first miracle, I have always maintained that if this Higher Power (which I now call God) was strong enough to take away my uncontrollable urge to drink, it was also capable of mending all those other lives of mine that I had irrevocably destroyed.

Added to this, the instantaneous disappearance of my sickening obsession and the spectacular recovery of all my lives is scientifically improvable:

1. No doctor can explain my good physical health following the sort of life I had led.
2. No psychiatrist can understand how I was able to overcome my demented behavior.
3. No psychologist can comprehend the quick recovery of my mental abilities.
4. No human resources specialist can understand my rapid rise to the top of my profession.
5. And finally, the absence of my physical allergy to

alcohol and of my mental obsession with drinking remain inexplicable phenomena for all those experts in the illness of alcoholism.

Upon my leaving the clinic, my parents allowed me to stay with them in order to keep me from returning to my old haunts. That served to help me over a difficult transitional period, since I had no money, no job, and no place to stay. I had a new AA sponsor, whom I had gotten to know during my cure at Domrémy, and since he had a car, I was able to attend a great number of AA meetings, sometimes up to ten a week. Of course I went back to the Cote-des-Neiges group, where I had been welcomed the first time and, at my sponsor's suggestion, I became involved in the group's activities. I took on the responsibility of preparing coffee for the members every Tuesday night.

Time passed quickly. My twenty-four hour periods of abstinence began to accumulate. I was presented with my three months of sobriety medallion. Unbelievably, my urge to drink did not return. I felt at peace with myself and with others. I undertook the AA's Twelve-Step Recovery Program, with the help of my sponsor and the veteran members of the groups that I attended. I asked my AA friends if it was still possible for me to find a job, given my truly dismal employment history. The answer wasn't long in coming: "André, you keep saying that it was impossible for you to stop drinking, but the moment you had the humility to ask God for help, your urge to drink disappeared. So show some faith and ask again."

It is so true. If God has the power to take away my infernal thirst, He can do anything for me. Now every time I take on something new, I ask Him to be with me and to choose what is good for me.

I resolutely began my job search and went down to the National Employment Office, where I used to work at the beginning of the nineteen-sixties. I made an application at the special employment section reserved for the physically handicapped and war veterans. The person in charge knew me (having once been a student of mine) and he said to me: "Well hello, André. What are you doing here? As far as I know, you are neither handicapped nor a veteran, so?"

"Well, Claude, I am in a way: you can recognize my handicap by the fact that I am an alcoholic undergoing rehabilitation, and I am greatly in need of assistance in returning to the job market. You yourself were a witness to the destruction of my career when I worked here and was your association president; so, can you help me?"

Claude was astonished, but his smile gave him away. He seemed happy to see me and, without a moment's hesitation, he answered. "Yes, I see, so I believe you when you say you are handicapped. In your case there is no doubt whatsoever. Your job history is really convoluted and almost impossible for any employer to swallow."

"Thanks for your understanding, Claude. Have you any suggestions for me?"

"Yes. Listen. . . . There's a public utilities company that's looking for customer service reps. They have an urgent need for workers, so you might slip through in the crowd. I'll schedule your appointment for next week. Take care and good luck!"

"Thank you so much, Claude. I'll let you know how it turns out."

A week later I went for my selection interview at the personnel services office. I wasn't even nervous, and the personnel officer offered me the job starting the following Monday. Incredible! I had a permanent job the first time that I applied for one: how easy! I have to admit, however, that at my sponsor's suggestion, I had asked God to help me have a good interview. That had worked like it would continue to in the future for many other interviews, as I was trying to rebuild my career. I had only stopped drinking for

117

a few weeks and look at me. I was in a job answering customer complaints!

It was very hard for me to say that a client was right, since for years it had been I who was always right, who had always sought, in my utter vanity, to have the last word. Since I was working on a three-month trial basis, my arrogance might damage my chances and put me at risk of losing my job if I couldn't improve the quality of my relations with the public. The supervisor who monitored new workers like me, had me listen to certain conversations with my clients that he had recorded. I noted a lot of aggression in my tone of voice and pretentiousness in my conversation. He then warned me: "You see, André, in the position you hold, the customer is always right."

"Yes but. . . . "

"Even if they're wrong, you have to avoid a confrontation; I didn't once hear you say to a customer that he was right!"

"Okay . . . I'll try to improve my ways."

That night at the AA meeting, I complained to my sponsor about my job and how I considered my position somewhat "junior" for someone like me. He understood me: "You poor guy, André, you should be overjoyed to have gotten a job so quickly. So now be happy with your 'junior' position for a while. Who do you think you are? Have you forgotten that a few months ago you were on the street?"

And wham! I quickly got myself back on track to becoming more humble. My sponsor went even further: "You know, André, the position you have will help you to work on your greatest weakness, your pride, buddy, your pride!"

With the trial period over, my supervisor called me to his office to inform me of the results of my evaluation for the first three months: "André I've decided to put you on probation for another three months because I've noticed a certain improvement in your work since we last talked; but if you don't continue to improve I'll have to let you go when this period is up."

I had just made it! Thank you, God! . . .

"And another thing, André, I checked your job application form and made a few inquiries; your references are doubtful, to say the least. Tell me what is a university graduate like you doing in a low-end job like this?"

"Thank you, sir, for giving me another chance. You won't regret it, I can assure you."

Then I told him about my progress in AA and how, because of my alcoholism, I had to start at the bottom rung in order to relaunch my career and rebuild my reputation. Touched by my honesty, he shook my hand and I felt that he had become an ally.

I continued my regular attendance at AA meetings, and I got involved in the groups' activities. My sponsor and the other members were of great assistance in helping me work on my weaknesses, and I quickly progressed along the path of the twelve-step program. The weeks passed quickly. I was coming to the end of my second three-month probation period, and my superior once again called me to his office. He had me listen to a new recording of my conversations with customers. I no longer recognized myself. I had become much more polite, my tone of voice had softened, and on a number of occasions I heard myself say to customers that they were right! My supervisor was overcome: "Can you tell me, André, how you could so rapidly and radically change your way of relating to your customers?"

"I would say that I gave it my best shot, and the help from my friends in AA made a big difference."

"Well, hats off to you! I confirm that you are now a permanent employee, and I am going to give you a raise in pay."

After congratulating me one more time, he let me know that the personnel officer who had hired me had been fired because he had not verified my job history or my references. The ways of God are sometimes very mysterious. For me to get my first job, some other person had to neglect his work and lose his job. How strange!

The days went by, I received my medallion for six months of sobriety, and I continued to be actively involved in the AA movement. The day I had stopped drinking was almost the same as my birthday. I decided to have my cake for one year of sobriety with the Cote-des-Neiges group where I attended my first meeting. What a great joy to make it that far! The group's members surrounded me, showing their affection and appreciation as they celebrated my accomplishment. At home my mother was overjoyed to see me healthy again. As for my father, he wasn't yet able to believe that I had succeeded in remaining abstinent all that time. He thought that I was still drinking in secret, and that, sooner or later, I would fall back into an alcoholic haze. He was always spying on me and making sure that I had repaid my mother all the money she had lent me, which I had done a long time ago.

Whenever I had a coffee or a cola, he would fire: "I see that you are still looking for drugs in another form, caffeine, or whatever God knows what. Can't you just drink water like everyone else?"

It was obvious that my father's attitude was really getting to me and was threatening my ability to stay sober with this sort of haranguing. It would soon be necessary to leave home before my resentment and my anger made me lose my newly acquired stability. I still needed a few more weeks to save a bit of money, and then I would find a way to move out for good.

At the age of thirty-seven, I couldn't, in any event, stay attached to my mother's apron strings indefinitely, and it was coming time for me to begin thinking about flying on my own. My sponsor suggested that I be very careful concerning my love life. He reminded me that each time I met a woman I would lose control of my emotions and have to take a drink to calm my nerves. He advised me: "Ask God to let you meet a woman who wouldn't be a danger to your sobriety."

Ah! If only I could get back the only woman I had loved with a true love at the level of the soul, with a love that inspired serenity and needed no support from alcohol. Claudette, where are you, my love? But this love was only an illusion. How could I dare to hope for such a meeting? I, who had destroyed everything with my savage and irresponsible behavior. I should force myself to forget Claudette, to leave her in peace, to live her life because I had no right to hurt her again by trying to find her and talk to her. No, Dear God, allow me to meet another woman. so that I may have some semblance of a normal life. That evening I would go to the Ahuntsic group meeting that needed my support, and there I would meet the person who would share my life for many years.

Decidedly, God acted fast! He had me meet a woman who seemed the answer to my emotional needs, but I soon found out that my interpretation of divine intervention was slightly mistaken.

This woman, whom I shall call Louise (in order to preserve her anonymity), arrived at the AA meeting in an advanced state of inebriation and somewhat disturbed everyone. I became well aware that she was very sick, both physically and psychologically. She shouted to everyone that she wanted to end it all, that she wanted to commit suicide that weekend. I went up to her and tried to explain the AA methods, but it was useless. She smelled of alcohol and her handbag was filled with all kinds of medications. Well dressed, despite a hat as oversized as her cigarette holder was long, she spoke using pretentious psychological jargon and judged the movement's members to be badly educated beer drinkers who were suffering from a sick sort of exhibitionism:

"I have never drunk beer nor engaged in profanity."

"But, Madame," I said, "it isn't a question of the quality of what you drink that makes you an alcoholic because, first and foremost, our sickness is located at an emotional level, and the kind or the amount of alcohol and the swear words used have nothing to do with our problem."

Louise was evidently not in a state to be able to understand anything. She began to cry and dashed out the door while shouting that she was going to the hotel to get good and drunk one last time before killing herself. Feeling responsible for her reaction to my speech, I ran after her and caught up to her in the middle of the street, where I led her back to the sidewalk before she could be hit by an oncoming vehicle. I tried my best to calm her down by telling her there were other groups that were of a higher class where people were better educated and more cultivated and more at her "level." I gave her my name and telephone number and made her promise to call me before she attempted suicide.

At home my father continued to harass me and question my sobriety. Nevertheless, everyone seemed to agree that I was in the process of changing and greatly improving my behavior in many spheres of my life. Even if I understood that my father mistrusted my rehabilitation because of all the many betrayals that I had him undergo, I was beginning to find his attitude extremely irritating! And that might threaten my sobriety since if I blew up and lost control of my emotions, I knew that there was a chance I might go and drink. I asked God to help me resolve this problem before it was too late.

A week after my meeting with Louise, she telephoned me to say that she was committing suicide the next day: "As promised, I am calling you before going for good. I have all the pills I need to end this once and for all."

I had no reason to doubt her intentions, and I tried to convince her to postpone her act and to give the AA method a second chance.

"You've got nothing to lose, Louise." I said to her, "Wait a few days more, and I'll take you to another meeting before you decide to use this ultimate means of making your escape."

After arguing for more than an hour, she finally agreed to my suggestion to visit another AA group on the following evening, and there she discovered people from all levels of society, such as doctors, lawyers, and other professionals. Louise was enchanted to finally meet alcoholics from her own social status, which satisfied her snobbish tendencies. During that same week, I met with her almost every day, introducing her to the most "chic" groups in the city's west end while observing the behavior of this walking suicide case. I decided to take care of this woman and used all means necessary to save her. There I was, assigned to a most important mission!

In the meantime my sponsor asked me if this was she, the woman whom I had asked God to have me meet. I needed nothing more to begin to dream about, leaving my parents' place having found the woman who would help me to recover an emotional life that was close to normal. But to say emotional life is to say love, at the very least, but I wasn't in love. I knew, above all, that I had a feeling of convivial empathy for this woman, a kind of feeling that AA members sometimes showed for each other.

Since my situation at home was becoming unbearable, I decided to tell my parents that I was going to live with this woman and that the normal thing to do for someone my age was to have his own home and family. To resolve my problem with my father, I once again became a galley slave. This time it would last more than twenty-five years. When would I learn that you don't get married to escape your father? It was the second time I had become involved without any real love in a relationship destined to fail from the very beginning.

I won't describe here all the double-dealing that such a relationship produced for both of us. But each time I was about to break off that crippled union, a tragedy would come along and prevent me from leaving this woman whom I had married on false and loveless pretenses. Quarrels with her and her children were present from the start, and when I first thought about going, her son died in an accident at the age of sixteen. It wasn't the proper moment to leave her while she was suffering so. Other times brought one serious event after another. There were heart attacks, major problems with her children (from a previous marriage), and on it went.

So at that point, I became resigned to accept what I couldn't change and escaped into my work and my pastimes. To satisfy my lack of affection, I took on all sorts of activities that provided some compensation and helped me forget for a while the recovery of that most important aspect of my life, a real love that I had always dreamed about and that now seemed impossible to find. I asked God to keep me sober despite these obstacles, and I gave myself to Alcoholics Anonymous, accepting any number of duties. This way, by helping others, I was able to forget my own problems, at the same time enjoying a serenity that I had never experienced before.

After some more years of sobriety, I became even more involved in AA and I started a new group in the Saint-Vincent-de-Paul penitentiary. Other members followed my lead by creating new chapters within the walls of other penal institutions. I continued to follow the twelve steps recovery program that AA advised, which helped me greatly to discover and work on my weaknesses. Pride is my major enemy, and I always have to avoid the traps that it sets for me. Also, the ninth step requires that "one should repair all the damage one has caused and directly make amends to those one has wronged wherever possible, except, when to do so, would injure them or others." So the list of individuals whom I had wronged was fairly long!

I will refrain here from providing an exhaustive account of the many direct amends that I had to make, but let me describe to you a few of them, to illustrate this step. After reimbursing my mother for all the costs that she had incurred while covering me for all my acts of fraud and stupidity, I resolutely took on the list of all my other creditors without further delay.

The first place I visited was the Café André, where I had drunk for so long and where I had left unpaid bills and NSF checks to the sum of approximately eight-hundred dollars. When I entered the café, the barmaid saw me and seemed quite shaken: she thought that I had died of cancer a long time ago, but she recognized me and called the owner: "Sir, there's someone who has come back to see you, Captain André M. of the USAF, do you remember him?"

The other end of the line went silent, then: "No, it can't be true. Isn't that guy dead? Oh, well, have him come up to my office."

I was a bit worried how the man to whom I owed so much money would react; how would he respond to my visit?

"Hello, sir. I have come to ask your forgiveness for the fraud I have committed and to make restitution for what I owe you."

He barely let me finish speaking, got up, gave me a big hug, and exclaimed: "Dear André, if you only knew how happy I am to see you in such good shape. So tell me what's happened to you?" I gave him a short history, my journey into hell and I got out my checkbook.

"How much do I owe you?"

"Put your check book back in your pocket. You don't owe me a thing. I made enough money off you in the good times, and I would feel ill at ease in accepting your offer. All is forgiven. How would you like a steak dinner? Let's go down to the restaurant and celebrate!"

On another occasion, I met a taxi driver who had ferried me from one hotel to another in the Deux-Montagnes County. In those days I would pay the driver with rubber checks of an amount that was always higher than what I owed for the trip, with the objective of getting enough cash to keep drinking. He too was quite shocked to see me arrive at his place on a bright Sunday, well dressed and completely sober.

"Good day, sir. I know I've owed you money for a long time, but I haven't come before now for reasons that you are certainly aware of."

Without saying a word, he opened his strong box and pulled out a stack of worthless checks that he had kept; they came to a total of two hundred and forty dollars, not counting those I had already repaid from time to time while I was still drinking. I wrote him a check for two hundred and fifty and, to satisfy my curiosity, I asked him: "But why then did you take my checks when you very well knew they were no good?"

"My dear sir," he replied, "if I had refused to take them, you might have killed me, you were so violent at the time! Believe me, I had no other choice!"

The righting of my past wrongs gave me great comfort, while restoring my confidence in my ability to become someone who was increasingly responsible. I expected to be the target of many accusations and much blame, but the vast majority of my creditors welcomed me with kindness, which allowed me to undo my feelings of guilt, at least as far as the material damage that I had inflicted because of my alcoholism. Unfortunately, I couldn't repair the most serious outrage I had committed, the one against the only love of my life, Claudette.

Already, by letting her go without any explanation, by destroying all her hopes (as well as my own), I had done her the greatest wrong. Now that I knew she was married and was surely happy with her children, I would be very unwelcome if I reopened her wounds while making my direct amends. This guilt and remorse would continue to haunt me for a long time to come. My sponsor urged me to forgive myself the offense that I had committed against Claudette, but I couldn't and I had to put myself in God's hands in order to find the strength to forget the worst moment in my emotional life.

If I couldn't conveniently re-establish my love life, my professional life was another story entirely. After more than two years as a junior clerk, with a salary of seventy-two dollars a week, I asked my sponsor if it wasn't time for me to try to progress a bit in my career development.

I believed that I had sufficiently regained my self-confidence to try to climb a few levels in the work world. My sponsor answered my question in a prudent but positive way: "Yes, André, you really can try for a higher-level position that would be more appropriate to your training. But watch out for your pride. Don't progress too fast because you know how easy it is for an 'alky' to lose his balance. I suggest that you look for a position as an assistant manager to gradually test your competence while avoiding those highly stressful situations that might compromise your sobriety."

Beginning on that day, I asked God to open the way for me and to help me find those jobs that were compatible with my level of sobriety. Having totally destroyed my reputation in the business world, I knew that it would take another miracle for me to return to my profession. The first miracle that made my thirst disappear sustained my faith in this God who could accomplish anything because He had done the impossible. He would, in the future, be in all my undertakings.

Following the publication of a job offer in the paper for the position of Assistant Director of Industrial Relations, I sent my C.V. off to the address indicated. It was a post office box number, and the ad made no mention of the employer's

127

name. Six weeks later I received a call from the Transport Commission requesting that I come for an interview. If I had known the employer's name, I would never have sent in my C.V., realizing that I had no chance of being accepted at the commission.

That evening I met one of my sponsors and told him what had happened: "Maurice, do you think I should go for the interview? You know, at the commission they check absolutely everything. They go as far as taking your fingerprints and dig into your past. I have no chance of getting this job . . . What do you think?"

"André, your faith should show itself in your actions and whatever you think, you should stay confident, keep 'rowing' and leave the destination to He who guides you. I strongly suggest that you go to the commission and ask God for a good interview. Even if you don't get the job, at least you will have had the audacity and the courage to go all the way."

Armed with this good advice, my faith strengthened by the memory of the preceding miracles, I made my way to the commission offices in complete confidence. Arriving at my destination, I was walking down a hallway toward the interview room when suddenly someone tapped me on the shoulder: "Hello, André. Is that really you? Remember me? I'm Jacques. I was your program supervisor when you were in your last year of university; but what are you doing here?"

"My God, Jacques, you haven't changed a bit. What have you been doing all this time? It must be over fifteen years since we last met."

"I'm now the Director of Industrial Relations at the Commission."

"And I have come here to be interviewed for the position of your assistant!"

Jacques grabbed my arm and led me into his office while reminding me what a good probationer student I was and how I also used to be his bridge partner. He asked me If I still played, if I liked golf, hunting and fishing and other things. The interview didn't have a lot to do with the position I was applying for because Jacques had already decided to hire me without further ceremony.

I had managed to short circuit the whole hiring procedure, and I had avoided all the usual background checks about my previous employment. The only thing remaining was my medical examination and with that, I would have passed the last hurdle. My faith was rewarded. Please excuse me for using the word "miracle" again, but I have no other term for it. The only thing that Jacques saw in me was this brilliant student who had an unlimited potential, and he decided to hire me. . . . Thank you, God!

I left the commission offices still in a state of shock about what had happened to me, I felt that I might lose control of my emotions, and that could be dangerous for my equilibrium and my sobriety. I didn't take any chances, and I called my sponsor:

"Maurice, hello, you'll never guess what happened. I've been hired at the Commission. And I'm so nervous and excited that I'm afraid I might go and take a drink to calm myself down."

"Come to my office right away. I'll try to reassure you a little."

Thanks to my sponsor's listening and his good advice, I was able to regain my composure and control my nervousness. I have to say that I had good reason to be nervous. How could I succeed in a job like that since I had never really worked in industrial relations? All I had was a diploma that I had received fifteen years earlier while I was drinking. That I had passed my exams was only due to my great memory. So I had no time to lose. I took out my textbooks and my notes from university. I went and read the most recent publications in the field, and I eagerly studied the Labor Code in order to prepare myself as quickly as possible to take over my new functions as Assistant Director of Industrial Relations at the Commission. Without God's help, I could never have risen to the challenge.

Faith and confidence helped. I was a great success in the position that I held as I took double helpings in my studies, working as fast and as hard as any good alcoholic could. It was such that barely two years after I returned to my profession, news of my successes began to get around in the business community, and I began receiving job offers without having to go to look for them. My reputation was on the way to being rebuilt. I could now be optimistic about my career and my whole future. I continued to attend AA meetings on a regular basis and helped other alcoholics with their recovery.

In this wonderful association of men and women, the last step to recovery reads as follows: "As a result of these steps, we have experienced a spiritual awakening and we will try and carry this message to other alcoholics and practice these principles in all our affairs." So "carry the message" means to go and tell the story of one's life with alcohol and to describe one's recovery with the help of the people in AA. For many years now, whenever I am asked to share the message with different groups (there are hundreds), I never say no. I owe so much to this association that I could never do enough to pay back all I have received. I owe them my new life, my resurrection. Among the many conferences I gave, let me describe just one.

One Sunday afternoon, the president of a group asked me to share my message to help celebrate the group's tenth anniversary. The meeting took place in a church basement on Robin Street, a few hundred steps from the Milano Tavern! As soon as I came into the room I was welcomed by a woman who cried: "My God, it's André, it's the Indian! Impossible! Well! Believe you me, if André has stopped drinking, then anyone can!"

This woman was the owner of the rooming house

where I had pretended to be an Inca prince!

Sober for over ten years, she hugged me around the neck, tightening her arms around me while weeping with joy. I was very touched by her show of affection, and I told her that I had been sober for over four years. To add to that there were two ex-bartenders from the Milano in the room who had since become AA members. They were Ben and Roger, and the latter had served me my last six beers that very special Saturday when God had taken my thirst away forever. But the most marvelous thing of all was when I saw "Tonton," who was attending his first AA meeting! I went up to him, he gave me his dirty and trembling hand and said: "Jeese, yer suppos'd ta be dead. What the Christ're ya doin' here?"

I didn't say a word, and I held him to my breast, this final witness to my misery and that miraculous morning when I left my terrible inferno. It was a Sunday that I'll never forget.

After more than two years at the commission, where I had rapidly progressed and improved in my work, I began getting job offers from a number of headhunters. One day I had a call from one of them, offering me a position as personnel director for a large municipality in the Montréal region. I had a successful interview with the municipal council, and the mayor assured me that I had been chosen and that I would be hired shortly. Two weeks went by without any news, and I decided to call the headhunter to ask how my file was progressing.

"Unfortunately, André, there was some political gamesmanship going on, and another candidate has been hired. I was just about to call you to let you know."

I found the situation a bit suspect, but I had to accept this setback. When I got home, my wife was furious and couldn't accept what had happened.

"It's not fair. You should get the job. They promised."

"Don't worry about it," I said, "It wouldn't have been

good for me; that's why I didn't get it."

A week later, the same headhunter called to offer me another position as the personnel director in an internationally-known research institute. I agreed to meet with the director general, and I was almost hired on the spot. I learned afterwards that my executive placement friend had managed to kill two birds with one stone: he had convinced the former personnel director to move from the research institute to the municipality where he had the contract while getting her order to fill the now vacant position.

A month later, when I was already working at the Institute, I was reading the paper and was struck by a news article: the firefighters and police officers from the municipality where I had failed to get the job as personnel director were now on strike! Thank you, God, for having once again protected me by keeping me away from a position that had quickly become a hornets' nest. When I didn't get the job in that municipality, it was because God had something better in reserve for me.

For all practical purposes, I pursued my career at the Institute for seven years in complete tranquillity while continuing to hone my skills in collective bargaining and human resources' management. I took the opportunity to enroll in a number of courses to upgrade my qualifications, and among others I obtained a certificate in labor law from the Université de Montréal. In both my professional association and in the business community at large, I became recognized as an innovator and an agent of change in the field of industrial relations. That led me to become Chairman of the Training Commission of my professional association. I was very, very motivated to make up for all my lost years, and the momentum created by my enthusiasm continued to increase along with my self-confidence and my faith in this God that never failed to grant me all that was good for me.

In addition to my work and my AA activities, I used my

leisure time to enjoy sports and I gave myself over to fishing in the Laurentians. My financial situation became healthy, which allowed me to travel on occasion. Being hyperactive, I was always looking for new challenges, and I decided to become concerned for the environment. I started a number of proprietors' associations for the purpose of fighting water pollution in the lakes of the upper Laurentians; I was actively involved in this work for about ten years. This activity led me to found two small local pollution information journals and got me elected as a municipal councillor. With the help of the teams that I had organized, we were able to clean up a good dozen lakes in Labelle county. It's almost impossible to believe that after only four years of sobriety, I had succeeded with God's help and AA's to be respected again. My physical and mental health had recovered, my professional life was on course to succeed, my financial situation had improved, and I had a small adopted family. Only my love life was escaping me, but I couldn't ask for too much. After all, barely four years ago, I had been a vagrant on the edge, totally lacking in human dignity, and now I owned a house, a summer cottage, a car, I had an interesting job, and my SOBRIETY! At this point in my life, I seriously believed that God had almost given me everything and that nothing else could be added to the joys that I had received.

There remained only one great emptiness to fill: the true love that I was looking for, THE encounter with my soul mate, my twin soul.... Would I find her?

In the meantime, married life with Louise had its ups and downs. The birth of grandchildren compensated somewhat for our lack of love as a couple.... Who knows? Perhaps God had let me meet this woman to teach me about certain aspects of married life that I had yet to understand. At any rate, I am certain that this situation helped me to have more acceptance of the things that I couldn't change for the present, and this was the positive side of the relationship which my sponsor tried to get me to see.

Anyway, should my obsessive thirst come back to haunt me, all I had to do was to open the drawer where my shirts are stacked. There, halfway down the pile, I could find the photograph of the Prince of the Incas staring up at me! Surely with that, my dreadful thirst would be quenched right away or dry up in shock!

Concerning my relationship with my father, the atmosphere between us became far more relaxed and we were able to resume talking and arguing on a normal basis. In 1973 struck by cancer, he lived his last moments in my presence, and he left this world while I held his hand as I told him that I loved him. Not being able to speak with his breathing tube in place, he squeezed my hand, forgiving me with that show of fatherly love.

6

Beyond Hope

At the time of my ten years of sobriety, I thought that I had received all the "dividends" that this new life of abstinence could bring me, and I asked God to simply help me keep what I had gained.

I had only to put my love life in order, but I was willing to wait and trust the matter to Him, concluding that perhaps I wasn't quite ready, taking my emotions into account, to meet my twin soul.

Every year that passed brought new challenges to my professional life well beyond anything I had hoped for. Imagine a little: to go from being a vagrant to a director in less than five years. And that was only the beginning! Even though I didn't make an intense effort to capture any prestigious positions, I received some surprising job offers. It was thus that I became, in turn: the deputy director general of an important financial institution, the vice-president of a food giant, and the vice-president of a large Québec manufacturing company. If you find this unbelievable, you're right . . . but, it happens to be true!

My parents, my friends, and everyone else who had witnessed my destruction, and the shameful state of my former lives, also could not believe their eyes. Some of them congratulated me for showing so much "will power" to stay sober, which actually had nothing to do with my recovery. No, my sobriety didn't belong to me, it was a gift of God's grace that I received. And I carefully looked after it by putting the AA program into practice and by sharing my life experience with others.

The image and the memory of Claudette often came to mind, and I also asked myself if she had seen all those photos of me that had been in the newspapers for each of my appointments. But I had to chase that mirage from my mind and forget the impossible dream that I might some day have her back.

My relationship with my wife did not get any better and slipped into a somber ongoing lovelessness; but perhaps I was too demanding, in that God had almost given me everything from the time when He had banished my thirst. I kept active in AA, which led me to carry my message presentation to many groups across the province. Obviously I would, while sharing my story, talk about Claudette, whom I had treacherously cast aside after having asked her to marry me. This did not help me to forget her in the least: in fact it was the opposite. I still felt a deep remorse, since in this case, I could not ask her to forgive me and make direct amends, for fear that old wounds would be reopened once again causing her more pain. So I had to live with my guilty conscience.

I had thus remedied all the other faults of my past, but it was impossible for me to correct the most serious, the one that had hurt me the most. My sponsor had done his best to convince me by saying over and over again that "No one is expected to perform impossibilities"; but that wasn't enough to remove the sadness and regret that I felt concerning this haunting memory of my cruel breakup with Claudette.

In spite of this setback in my love life, I continued to develop other aspects of my return to normal. I wrote a lot and I published a booklet on "Human Resources as a Corporate Function." which was published and distributed through my professional association. I organized conferences and seminars and was often invited to give presentations on diverse aspects of the world of industrial relations for other members of the business community. I was thus fulfilled in my other lives, and I had a vague intuition that somehow, one day soon, my love life would also be addressed. For the time being I was obliged to leave it in God's hands and stop worrying about it. I associated with the business elite and the top professionals of Montréal and Québec City, and everything went by so fast that I had no time to feel sorry for myself.

From time to time, because of my dark past, strange and awkward situations would arise making me aware of just how much sobriety could change one's life. One of my best examples of this sort goes like this: One day, while attending a board of directors meeting for a large supermarket chain (where I was a vice president), a member of the board began praising me to the skies for having negotiated a collective bargaining agreement without having a strike. He kept calling me "sir" as if I had just been knighted and could not stop complimenting me. However, this was the same supermarket owner who, fifteen years earlier, had kicked me out of his store, making me wait outside because he thought I was too dirty! Oh, yes! I was this guy who delivered his advertising flyers. He never recognized me, and I had to stifle my laughter. . . . If he had only known whom he was talking to. But he would never know! I had gone from being the poor slob whom he had chased out the door fifteen years before and had now become his idol. Thank you, God!

My economic life reflected my career progress, and my financial condition allowed me to live a life of ease in better and better surroundings, in sharp contrast to my last years of drinking when I either slept outside or in an abandoned van. After one year of sobriety, I treated myself to a furnished one and a half room basement apartment in a building on Place d'Acadie, mice and roaches provided, for a total of eighty dollars a month (heat included).

After two years of abstinence, I went up a notch and rented a three and a half room upper duplex and in less than four years, I had the means to buy a Maison Canadienne* in Laval to house my wife and her three children. In addition I bought a summer cottage in the Laurentians the year after that. Later I occupied some waterfront houses and when I accepted an important position in Québec City, I moved into a splendid house on a mountain side overlooking Lac Beauport. What a contrast to the life that alcohol had given me.

As for the "material" aspect of my life, I was completely satisfied and I had a hard time believing that everything that had happened to me was real. My extraordinary metamorphosis left my family and friends utterly amazed. But my love life had not gotten any better, and the gulf continued to grow between my wife and myself. I met many fabulous women, but I was unable to find that "rare jewel" who could awaken that feeling of true love within me, this one and only unquestionable feeling. None of these women made my heart beat and my soul sing like my feelings for Claudette that had positively thrilled me so. I was convinced that when I had declared to her that I would love her forever, I had spoken the truth, as the song goes: "Once love I, always love I."

The good life continued without any real setbacks up to the time when my position was eliminated. I found myself jobless at fifty-four, and I had to sell my fine house in Lac Beauport and return to Montréal. Luckily, the severance package offered by the company allowed me to live comfortably for at least another year without having to dip into my retirement fund. But losing one's job at that age could cause serious problems since it would be hard to find another position at the same level, not only because of my age, but also because of the economic recession at the time.

*A cottage with curved gable roof and dormer windows

My wife was in despair and refused to accept that I was taking things so calmly. I increased my AA activities having more time to devote to them and helped those who needed it. As my faith had not weakened, I sincerely believed that my God had not brought me that far just to simply let me down so abruptly. I had confidence in life and a premonition that sooner or later this God of love would show Himself once again and save me with another of His mysterious graces. What were His intentions for me? I didn't know, but I was sure that my faith would not betray me, and I kept thinking that if He had been able to banish my thirst, He could present me with another miracle, no matter what. While waiting for this "surprise," I was self-employed as a consultant while sending out my C.V. to the headhunters in Montréal.

Because of my "advanced age," fifty-four, I had only a few encouraging replies. I received piles of polite letters in praise of my abilities, the kind that said: "We appreciate your interest in this position, but we find that you are professionally overqualified for the job." I knew that they were politely telling me that I was too old. My friends sympathized with me and many indicated that they didn't hold out a lot of hope for me because of the existing economic situation and the few positions that were available in the job market. Then, one day, after ten months without results, I got a call from a woman headhunter who wanted me to apply for the position of vice-president in a service enterprise, the same place where I had first been hired twenty years before, as a customer services rep!

Ten days later I found out that I was tied for first place with another candidate but, given my age, I didn't get the job. Thank you, God, since at least I was still able to end up near the top. My wife took it very badly; she was quite insecure and didn't have the same faith as I did in divine providence. I assured her that if I didn't get the job, it probably would have been a bad one for me, reminding her of the time when I wasn't chosen for the risky position as a municipal personnel manager. But she had no faith in me and accused me of being contented with my indolence. This woman would certainly never understand me. Our relationship continued to deteriorate, and there was more and more growing resentment. About two months later, the same executive placement consultant called me to ask if I would be interested in applying for an upper management job at an industrial relations research institute where the president was leaving.

"Their president is about to retire," she told me, "and since we are looking for someone with experience, preferably in their fifties and bilingual, we were thinking that your application might interest our client."

I immediately said yes to another interview and to the taking of a battery of aptitude tests. After surviving the preliminary selection process, I found myself on a short list of five applicants chosen to meet with the institute's board of directors for the final selection. The following week I was invited to a meeting of the board at the Mount Royal Club. The nine board members were present and asked me, in turn, numerous questions to test my expertise and probe how extensive my knowledge was. I could have been very nervous and stressed out, but before I went to the meeting I asked God to keep me calm and give me the help that I needed to have a good interview.

After my being grilled for two hours on the hot seat, my trial came to an end and I was left alone with the Chairman of the Board who was quite happy with my showing. He asked me my conditions and affirmed that he would recommend my appointment to the other members of the board. I had never aspired to become the president of anything in my professional life, and there it was, another surprising turn of events and, against all expectations, I was propelled to the height of my career at the same time as my situation seemed so hopeless. And again I repeat, that finding a job like that at the age of fifty-six, during an economic recession, was both a marvel and a mystery.

I was the Institute's president for the next nine years of my career where I was most happy to counsel and serve over three hundred member-companies comprising more than one million employees in Québec and across Canada. In less than twenty years of sober living, I had gone from the status of wandering flyer delivery man, unemployed vagrant, and human slug to a position of prestige as president of the leading organization in my profession. Even if I am credited with following my AA recovery program, even if I was able to work fast and hard to rebuild my reputation, I couldn't claim all this success for myself and I continue to remain convinced of a divine intervention. At each stage of this marvelous life that has been given back to me, this resurrection, this transformation can only be the work of a Power far beyond the talents that I have been blessed with.

At the time we lived in a splendid house on the waterfront at the Pointe du Moulin*on Ile Perrot. There I was able to participate in my favorite sport: fishing on Lake Saint-Louis and the Saint Lawrence River. It was one of my ways of getting out of the house where the situation with my wife was getting heavier and heavier. The other way I kept busy, in addition to my work, was to participate in charity work and to give much of my time to the Community Chest, the Red Cross and other social organizations. Working with other AA members, I participated in the creation of the "Starting from Zero Foundation" in order to raise funds for alcoholics and drug addicts who hadn't the financial means to go into treatment programs. These activities led me to organize golf tournaments, supper shows, dinner theater and other fund-raising events.

All this hyperactivity distanced me from home where an atmosphere of confrontation continued. Moreover, I

*Mill Point

kept giving talks for AA, and each time it would cause me to remember my past by reliving the memory of my love for Claudette, the love that I had destroyed because I was incapable of assuming it at the time.

My marriage continued to deteriorate, and I dreamed more and more about leaving my wife to find the peace and freedom that I had been lacking for such a long time. It was not that I had it in my head to go and live with another woman since I was unable to meet one who was capable of awakening the same feelings in me that I had felt for Claudette. Above all I dreamed of a half-solitary existence where I could immerse myself in reading, writing, and my other interests. I could also devote more time to volunteer work, to helping other alcoholics who were still suffering and to share the joys of my sobriety with them. But even so my subconscious mind kept sending me thoughts of Claudette to make me dream of these impossible encounters that could only eventually take place in my fanciful imagination.

In 1993, being about one year before I retired, I had to sell the cottage on Ile Perrot because my wife wanted to be closer to her children who lived in Montréal. I bought a home in Laval, and after a few months, I noticed that the children weren't calling to the house any more often even when a large heated swimming pool had been provided for them. The conflict between my wife and her children disappointed me and made our already shaky relationship even worse. Sooner or later, without a doubt, I had to leave this hornets' nest and recover the serenity that maintained my emotional equilibrium.

Actually, I could not take a chance on losing my sobriety much longer. Because of the mounting resentment I felt building within me, I knew that resentment could easily lead to hate, my emotional health's worst enemy, and therefore an enemy of my sobriety as well. Even though I had been sober for more than twenty-five years now, I was

142

still a fragile person and I knew my weakness whenever I lost control. Anger could easily lead me to actions with irreparable consequences, which was why it was vital and imperative that I find a realistic solution to the problem caused by a relationship with someone who was never really a wife to me. My union with her had been a marriage of convenience, and this convenience had ceased to exist long ago. I had to make a radical break from these false bonds that had been tied in the absence of love.

At the end of 1994, I retired from the Institute and decided to form a small consulting firm with a longtime friend. So I opened an office at my home in Laval and became self-employed, thus lessening the shock of a retirement that would cut me off from my professional activities too suddenly. My new life went relatively well for a time, and I had some contracts that were quite worthwhile and interesting. However there was a fly in the ointment since I was now condemned to live at home twenty-four hours a day, which stirred up the coals in the prevailing climate of hostility of our household. I couldn't so easily escape anymore into my work and my other activities as I had done before. And I found myself more often than not alone with my wife, and this had us arguing together almost every day. Without authentic love, there was no possible solution to our problem, and on many occasions in the past, one or the other of us had seriously wished to break it off. But circumstances, lack of courage, and the well-known excuse of "because of the children" were no help in ending it.

As I lived in Laval and no longer owned a cottage or a house on the waterfront, it was impossible for me to go fishing as often as I wanted to. But at the time I had sold the house in Ile Perrot, I had asked my mother to keep my boat at her cottage in Saint-Placide on the Lac des Deux-Montagnes. I went as often as I could to partake of my favorite sport of fishing. This enchanting place, where I had had the marvelous meeting with Claudette in 1957, allowed me to go back to my roots while retrieving the necessary amount of serenity to maintain my emotional equilibrium and my sobriety. Alone on my lake with God, I could make an almost concrete contact with Him, and I could almost feel His presence. I asked Him to give me the courage to find the remedy for my marital problems and to help me to a more normal love life, as He had done for the other aspects of my life.

In 1995 I put my house in Laval up for sale and began to look for a waterfront property to enjoy my well-deserved retirement. As my wife didn't want to be too far from Montréal, we focused our search around Lac Saint-Louis, Lac Saint-François and Lac des Deux-Montagnes. We looked at a number of properties without finding the ideal spot the first time and, after several months of unsuccessful looking, we targeted the Lac des Deux-Montagnes region with the help of a new real estate agent.

We made a conditional offer to purchase a lovely property located on Pointe-aux-Anglais,* near the town of Oka. But the owner had accepted a firm offer, and we lost our option to buy. It was the same for another offer to purchase in Saint-Placide Bay where the owner's sale price was not negotiable. Finally our real estate agent told us that his own house was for sale, and he already had one conditional offer for it. It was a dream house on the water's edge with a superb view overlooking the Lac-des-Deux-Montagnes. I jumped on the opportunity and there I was, the proud owner of the house of my dreams!

I closed up my office in Laval in the spring of 1996 and moved into my new home on a fine sunny day in April. The day after the move I was sitting with the lake before me and I watched the sunset colors on the little bay with its rays, the same bay where I had first met Claudette in 1957. Inevitably all my thoughts were invaded by that sweet

*English Point

memory, and I really wondered why I still kept hoping to meet this woman whom I had loved so much, once again, even after forty years of separation. Would God answer me that He had already put the pieces of the puzzle in place, one by one, to complete my destiny? I had a vague feeling that my life was about to change dramatically.

7

One Last Miracle

I had tried to avoid arguing with my wife, but my efforts became increasingly futile, communication had been cut off; the atmosphere in the house was so heavy that I had a hard time staying in the same room with her. In addition, I lived and slept in the basement, like a tenant in my own house. This couldn't go on for long because I began to be aware of feelings of hate growing inside me, and this made me afraid. My only remaining respite was to escape by going fishing when the weather permitted. Even then, I had to sneak out to avoid her accusations and her sarcastic comments. On my return, she scowled at me as if I had left her for days. I no longer felt at home, I experienced rejection and mistrust on a daily basis, and no matter what I said or did, I was always wrong.

The only exception to this rule was when we had visitors. At those times the empty facade prevailed, hiding every trace of marital conflict. Appearances had to be maintained on the pretext of a successful marriage! I didn't hold my wife solely to blame for our failed relationship since I too was at fault. However, our inevitable breakup was mostly due to our notorious incompatibility and the unavoidable awareness that a lack of real love was the root cause of our problem. I couldn't forget the fact that I had gotten married to leave home and to escape my father's influence. That was certainly not a good recipe for a long-lasting relationship.

Another way I had of staying away from the home that I was beginning to curse consisted of increasing my activity in AA. I was often being asked to share my experiences and to make presentations to many groups across the province. One day, while I was speaking at a meeting in Laval, I surprised myself by telling my audience: "I haven't finished my ninth step (which consists of making direct amends to those we have hurt), but this year, I have decided to try to remedy this by finding Claudette and asking her to forgive me, without hurting her at the same time. However, I am not so sure my wife will agree to my taking such an initiative."

It was the first time that I had said something like that in my address, and I really wondered what had come over me. Certain portents as well my intuition told me that God was preparing me to experience a profound change in my love life. That night I went to bed asking Him to light the path that I was to follow and, the next day, I had my answer.

It was June 1997, the month when God gave me the courage to make the firm decision to leave my wife. I would wait till October, after Thanksgiving, to tell her since I didn't want to wreck the celebration with her children and grandchildren. In the meantime I checked the classified ads section of the newspaper for a new house for the single person I wanted to become. I wanted to find a quiet spot by a small lake where I could immerse myself in fishing, meditation, and who knows, perhaps writing as well. My wife had no doubts that something was going on, but I tried to hide my intentions for the time being. I knew that when the time came to let her know that I was leaving, God would give me the courage I needed to withstand the tidal wave that this situation would cause. But I was certain that nothing would stand in my way, being already full of the spiritual energy that would help me make my transition into a new life. Yes, alone with God in His Universe, I would be now be freed from the yoke of a marriage that had become unbearable.

I took advantage of fine summer days to attend a number of AA meetings in and around Lachute, located about twelve miles from my residence in Saint-Placide. With Claudette being born in Lachute, I well knew that it was the best place to start my search and, eventually, to be able to make my direct amends, while making sure that I would not cause her any pain or grief. I had to find out her actual situation and not contact her unless circumstances allowed it. I had no wish to reopen old wounds if it would only serve to cause her additional suffering. My cruel desertion of 1957, without any explanation, was already a heavy enough burden for her.

I started to discreetly question the AA members in the Lachute region and found out that she was living in Hull and that she might have been divorced for some time. What great news for me! I had to try to get more information and, who knew, perhaps it might be possible for me to get in touch with her.

Despite some promising signs, I really didn't have any serious hope of seeing her again and even less of renewing any kind of a relationship with her. However, I would be perfectly happy to have the privilege of asking her to forgive me in order to end, once and for all, the remorse that had been gnawing at me for the past forty years. I often talked to my friends about my imminent breakup with my wife and I told them my big secret, that I had only ever loved one woman in my whole life and that woman was Claudette, the girl I met in Saint-Placide in 1957 beside the Lac des Deux-Montagnes.

I confided that my dream of one day being with Claudette again was impossible, in view of the hurt I had caused her in the past. But I was firmly committed to pursue my undertaking to the very end and to do everything I could to find her and ask her forgiveness. I began to think of her daily, and strange vibrations made themselves felt in all my being. It was as if Claudette was gradually approaching me before I had even made a move in her direction. . . .

My heightened state of excitement intrigued my wife, and when she caught me looking at the properties for sale in the classified ads on a fine Saturday on Labor Day weekend, and she asked me outright: "Will you please be so kind as to tell me exactly what is going on? You have been acting strangely for the past couple of weeks. Are you looking for another house without telling me? So what are you cooking up?"

My heart began beating rapidly. My emotions were crackling all over the place. Then all the repressed feelings burst into the open. There was an explosion of all the frustrations accumulated over the years that could not be silenced any longer. I didn't wait for Thanksgiving to be over.

I took my courage in both hands and let her have it: "I thought I might tell you later. But since you asked, I have decided to leave you and to go and live by myself. I can no longer stay here with you, and I have to leave before I start hating you, before I do something irreparably stupid, before I get the urge to kill you! I have made my decision, and I won't go back on it. We have no more reason to live together, nothing more to say to each other."

The room went deathly silent, and my wife couldn't believe her ears; she never thought I would have the strength to act like that and she shouted: "I can't believe what you are saying. So then, what's going to happen to me?"

"Above all, don't worry about it. I'll give you everything that you need to live quite comfortably. It's time for you to choose a lawyer!"

It isn't necessary to describe here all the disgraceful scenes that followed and all the efforts that she undertook to get me to change my mind. She even named certain women for me whom she thought I might be going away with. She tried to discover who my "mistress" was, even though I never, in all my life, had any such adventures. It was always easier to blame the other woman than look directly at the truth and admit one's wrongs. My wife's pride was wounded, and she couldn't accept the fact that I had been the one to make the first move and not her. Her anger was transformed into episodes of hysteria, speeding in her car and scenes of self-pity.

Certainly I too was prey to all sorts of emotions, which went from the joy of my coming freedom to the pain of cutting my ties to her children and grandchildren at the same time. It is evidently very difficult to just throw away more than twenty-five years of life experience. But I didn't have any choice, because if I stayed any longer, I was convinced that I might one day lose control, act inappropriately, and destroy myself. It was time to end this relationship that had become unlivable, seeing that such dreadful thoughts were occupying my mind.

Despite the upset caused by this separation, I tried to remain calm and I asked God to help my wife to understand the decision that I had made. I continued my involvement in Alcoholics Anonymous and, at the beginning of September, an AA member asked me to go and deliver my message to a group in Lachute.

The night of the meeting, I felt more nervous than usual. I had a stark premonition that something was going to happen, and my emotions were on the very edge of foreshadowing a very significant event. The chairman of the meeting made the usual introductions, and I went up to the podium to make my presentation. I had a hard time repressing my nervousness. I was overcome with stage fright as if this were the first time I had ever given a talk and I wondered what was happening to me.

Finally I succeeded in opening my mouth and stammered out: "Good evening, friends in AA, my name is

André, and I am an alcoholic." *Whew! I'm off.* I cleared my throat, I coughed, then regaining some composure, I began my talk, which would last about fifty minutes and would cover my life as a recovering alcoholic.

When I came to the part where I usually described my meeting with Claudette, the only true love of my life, and the brutal way that I had abandoned her, I went dumb. I was literally paralysed and the room was utterly silent. I had great difficulty controlling my tears. I was frozen in a feeling that reduced me to nothingness as if all the remorse, all the bitterness, and all the sorrow were coming to the surface after all those years of living in the pain and regret of losing Claudette forever. The few minutes that followed seemed an eternity.

I finally more or less managed to continue and was barely able to say: "Please excuse me, but I find it so very painful whenever I reveal this part of my life, that I break down. And tonight it is even harder since I am in the very town where we used to go out together and I almost feel as if she were here . . . "

After the meeting the members thanked me for my sharing, and one of them came up to me and asked: "Say, André, this Claudette that you speak so emotionally about, is she really a Lachute girl?"

"Yes, Mario, her name's Claudette Danis, and she used to live in Lachute."

"For sure, André, I knew your Claudette quite well. I used to go drinking with her brother."

"Tell me, Mario, do you know where she's living now? Do you have her address? Has she remarried?"

Questions were flying from everywhere, and I finally felt that I was on the right track.

"All I can say for sure, André," he answered, "is that she's divorced and presently living in Hull with her twin daughters. As far as her address is concerned, I'll try to get it for you."

I went back home to my place, and I had a hard time containing my feelings of joy. It took all my strength to hide this new energy that was surging within my soul. I went directly to the basement to avoid my wife's questions, and I took a nearly cold shower to try to calm down. It was useless; I didn't sleep a wink that night. I was now almost certain that I could write to Claudette to ask her forgiveness. What a gift! What happiness! Finally I could free myself from this burden that had weighed me down for so many years.

I tried all night to compose a letter asking my love to forgive me; after many tries I succeeded in drafting an outline of all my thoughts; but I was so bombarded by the force of my emotions that I was barely able to find the words to express what I hoped to say. I burnt all the notes that I had used to write this letter to keep my wife from finding out what was going on, and I carefully hid my final draft containing the heart of the message that I wanted to send to Claudette.

The next morning I went to Mario's place of business to find out more about her and especially to get her address. I was so excited that I literally blew into his office without bothering to knock or to apologize to him for disturbing the conversation that he was having with one of his customers. When his client left, Mario welcomed me with a smile and offered me coffee.

"Well, André, my friend, you sure seem to be in a hurry. I'm beginning to see how important it is for you to find that information."

"You've got that right, Mario. Presently it's the only thing that interests me!"

Then he told me that he had tried to get the information from a girlfriend of Claudette's, but she had refused to help out. I asked him if he knew her sister's address, the one who still lived in Lachute. He found it in the telephone directory, wrote it down on a scrap of paper, and then told me to how to get to her place. I was chomping at the bit, and I thought out my plan to send Claudette my request for forgiveness. I would meet with her sister and explain why I needed to do this, hoping that she would forward my letter.

After leaving Mario I hurried to the shopping center to buy a card in order to copy the final version of the text that I had prepared on to it. Having found what I wanted, I perched myself next to the counter of a little snack bar. While sipping a coffee, I wrote the famous note that was to be, without my knowing it, the means of setting unbelievable events in motion. But I was so nervous while doing this that I accidentally hit my cup and splashed coffee all over the counter, spraying the people around me. Luckily, the coffee missed the card that I was preparing and I made my apologies to those whom I had baptized.

I carefully reread my text, I felt I could do better: but time was running out and I had to get to Claudette's sister's place as soon as possible before mealtime came. Before arriving in Lachute, I had been very careful to put on my best suit with white shirt and tie so I could make a good impression with that sister of hers. I had no trouble finding the place and, shaking all over, I rang the doorbell once, twice, and then a third time. There was no answer. However, the windows were open and I could hear music playing; the neighbor informed me that they had probably gone to the hospital since their father was very ill. I decided to leave my letter in their mailbox, with the hope it might be sent on. . . .

In the meantime my wife had found a lawyer and I had to attend several meetings to finalize division of our property and assets as well as the apportionment of household effects.

While these painful negotiations were under way, the house was a living hell and my wife refused to do things in a civil manner. She became extremely dramatic as if we had loved each other forever. I prayed for her, and I sped up my search for a new place to live. I decided to meet with her two daughters to explain the situation to them, and they seemed to understand everything as if they had been expecting the breakup for a long time.

Since I had put my letter to Claudette in her sister's mailbox without explaining my reasons for doing so, I wondered if she had been willing to play the role of intermediary and if she had promptly forwarded my message. I was worried enough about the contents of this letter, not being certain that I had found the right words to really make Claudette understand the deeper meaning of my request for forgiveness. Once again I went over the draft of my text that I had kept and it read as follows:

Saint-Placide, September 16th, 1997

Hello Claudette,

I write you these words for three main reasons: to thank you for

1. Having saved my life one New Years Day (on a certain January first).

2. Introducing me to the Serenity Prayer and AA.

3. And to ask you to forgive me for the way I treated you in the past.

I have neither your address nor your telephone number, because I don't want to reestablish contact with you without your permission. If you agree, I will be most happy to talk with you by telephone. . . . Evidently, if circumstances permit, being able to see you again would fill me with happiness.

I ardently hope that you answer me with a short note with your sister's cooperation.

If you do not wish to reestablish contact with me, I won't insist and will (regretfully) accept your decision. I pray that you and I will meet again before we die.

Most sincerely, André

My brain was flooded with thousands of questions. *Was Claudette really living alone? How would she react to my request? Would she take it in the right way? Had I again made another mistake that would only serve to revive past suffering?*

My troubled mind prevented me from getting any rest, and the following nights would be almost sleepless. But, by asking God to grant it, I ended up being able to sleep for a few hours and my faith prevented my thoughts from being shrouded in darkness. Knowing her deeply generous nature, I was sure that she would forgive me. As for her agreeing for us to "meet again before we die," I had little hope, for that would take a miracle. . . . The days went by, and I kept my eye on the mailbox in case my wife might get her hands on the envelope before I did and discover Claudette's answer at the very time our separation was ongoing. I could only imagine her reaction. One that would set off another explosion of hurt and misunderstanding.

At the end of ten days of anguish, where hope and despair coexisted, I noticed that the flag on the mailbox was raised, and I hurried to go through the mail where I found a letter with a Hull postmark! I hid it inside my undershirt. It felt as if my heart had only beat once and I was short of breath! Since I had decided the night before to go fishing that morning, I jumped in my boat and almost tipped it. Then I started the outboard motor and nearly tore the handle off the starter cord as I aimed the boat for the center of the lake.

I was so excited that I felt my head would pound until it burst. I was sweating and my hands shook as if I had been drinking. When I was well out on the lake, I turned off the motor and let myself drift. I caught my breath a little, and putting my hand under my shirt, I pulled out the fateful letter and just about ripped it in two while opening it. Thus, with my heart at a standstill, with my soul in a turmoil, my eyes burning with the fire of first tears, I finally found the courage to read Claudette's answer; it was as if I were hanging between heaven and earth and I felt my spirit take flight as I read:

Hull, my home, first evening of autumn 97.

Good evening André,
   It is with respect that I accept your wish for forgiveness. This undertaking, which I imagine has been long and perilous, must have required courage and humility.
   Yes, André, I forgive you.
   I agree to see you whenever the moment seems right. In the meantime, I may be reached by telephone.
   May your life be what you desire and the choice of He who guides you.

                                   Sincerely, Claudette

A miracle! I, in the deepest recesses of my being, had so hoped to be able to one day obtain her forgiveness. Now it had happened, God had granted me this great happiness! But the most unexpected of these gifts was that Claudette was opening the door to an eventual meeting and that she had given me her telephone number! Never would I have once thought this possible, and I dared not believe my eyes. My heart was bathed in joy and I felt a kind of happiness that I never believed possible. I thanked God out loud on the open lake. I shouted, "Thank you!" at the top of my lungs and I feverishly reread over and over again the blessed words that Claudette had sent me. Experiencing such strong emotions led me to deeply reflect on the meaning, the interpretation that I should give to all that had happened to me and I wondered how coming events would unfold.
   I felt that I should quickly get in touch with her to fix a date for a meeting. But how would she respond to my strong feelings? I was so enthusiastic that I would have a hard time hiding the fact that I still loved her with all my

heart, and perhaps I might frighten her. I had to be careful and take all the time necessary to show her that my feelings for her were sincere. And there I was, coming on too fast, always too fast, taking my dreams for reality. Be calm, André, because you can still wreck everything. I tried to contain myself a little by taking a few casts on my fishing line, but my heart wasn't in it and the fish weren't biting. Not wanting to get home too soon, for fear that my excitement might betray me and raise questions with my wife, I passed some time trolling while bringing to mind the fine features of Claudette's beautiful face and the clear reflection of her soul in the sparkle of her eyes.

I came home and I more or less succeeded in hiding my feelings, to slow the heartbeat that was pulsing in my temples and taming the smile that was threatening to invade my cheeks.

That night I found it hard to sleep without starting to dream of Claudette's impossible return to my life. I was worried about the next step that I had to take. I really wondered how to begin our coming conversation on the telephone and how she would feel. Even if she had forgiven me with all the generosity that she possessed, how would she survive the memory of that painful past and my sudden and unexpected reappearance? It was only later that I learned how Claudette had reacted to my letter at that moment when she let me read what she had written at the time, in her diary.

Here are a few passages.

Upon Receiving His Letter

To reopen a wound
to relive the pain
of seeing love aborted
the purest love
I had ever known.

Immaculate love
in a young girl's heart
would be dissolved in thought,
would be muted in the face of absence,
   of the past.

Frights, fears.

Lying, hurt
Mixed with the will to love,
Passing out uncounted pain.

Burning the letters.
Giving away the ring
Was not enough
To erase his memory.

His memory anchored
in the first place of my heart
cut a deep furrow
where all my tears flowed.

The first love
encrusted for life
molds others to come.

I am afraid still,
I cry still.
More than my memory,
My heart recalls,
My reason can but only
Repeat my emotions ceaselessly
That rhyme not with reason.

An ever flowing spring of tears

At my heart's summit
Ends by making the dam break
By letting the pent up waters
Run in the passages of blood.
Tears, nothing but tears.

A world of tears where I swim
    against the stream.
This inconsolable river
That flows within me.

Eyes of salt water,
A heart too large,
A strangled cry,
A heart too full
That overflows, that groans.

This heart sails
In deep currents
That flow northward
and nothing can be done.
I soon pray to the waters

To give me an isle,
A rest, a repose.
I pitch, I tip,
I founder, it's too much to bear.

It was hell at the house. My wife was feeling rejected
and abandoned, and she continued to rebel against my decision, one that she knew to be irreversible. After a third
meeting with her lawyer, the legal document of "Amicable
Separation" was finally signed, and now the last obstacle to
my freedom had been removed. All the proceedings for the
division of property and assets had been completed before
my initiative to approach Claudette had been carried out,

Thus my decision to leave my wife had nothing to do with the events that followed.

I waited for the right moment when I would be alone (with no chance of being disturbed) to telephone and to hear Claudette's voice after forty years of silence and of being eaten up by emotional loneliness. Upon rereading her letter for the umpteenth time, trying to see in it a sign of hope or an afterglow of our past love, I finally decided to make the call, the most important one of my life.

"Good evening, Claudette, It's André. How are you?"

She was so overcome by emotion that I could barely hear her voice, her language had changed so much that I had a hard time recognizing her; I felt her torment; besides, she was just like me, too emotional to quickly engage in conversation. I was confused, she was so fragile that our first exchange of words was filled with long silences. Then, suddenly, there was a moment of unexpected humor, and the clear music of Claudette's laughter broke the ice between us and opened the floodgates for the torrents of our words! We briefly told each other the essential events of our lives. She confided that because of the pain I had caused her, she had burned my love letters and given my ring to her sister. That said, I quickly replied that I would present her with one that was even more beautiful!

Claudette informed me that her father was very ill, that she visited him regularly at the Lachute Hospital, and that next weekend on the fifth of October she would be at his bedside. I asked her if it would be possible to meet with her then, and she agreed without any hesitation. We would see each other again at 2:00 P.M. at the "Chez Carole" Restaurant on Main Street in Lachute. A thousand questions remained in our minds but, exhausted by our efforts to control the emotions that we could no longer hide, we said good-bye to each other and hung up. . . .

I was trembling all over, there was an opening, a veil had been lifted, letting me see a far off oasis. Was it a mirage? No, no, André, stop dreaming, slow down, put on the brakes, I was overcome by my blind attraction to this love that I could never ever forget. God help me!

I felt that my conversation with Claudette may have upset her and perhaps reawakened past feelings that she had thought were buried long ago. Following my call to her on September 30th, she described the swirl of her emotions in her diary: with her permission, I have included a few lines:

After His Phone Call

I have come back to find you
After forty years of silence.
I heard his voice, his hope,
He waits for me, and he wants me.
And I, I heard myself laugh.
This love is a force I cannot comprehend
Yesterday I cried out loud again.

I go on like a river
on the current of my destiny.
I go on like a tightrope walker
On the thread of time.
I have faith despite all belief,
This "thing" indefinable,
This penetrating force.
I go on, nearly singing
And yet, will this be chance?

I return to dream
Near colored woods.
I return again to dream.
I happen to believe in love
That asks for nothing, that lives in all.

I see myself happy, close to this man of mine.
He in whom I see myself,
He in whom I see a soul alive.
I see days of tenderness
Where time is in harmony with the
        rhythm of the days.
I see a hand held out
To welcome and to give,
A hand to go with, together.

Strangely, the pain seems past,
Feelings of hope revived.
Softly I ready myself to awake
To a yet-to-come of love and forever
In a misty land.
I see the unseeable,
The face of the man I loved
Who left me one day,
Love larger than we
Love larger than time.
It must he understood,
respected
welcomed
honored,
Awaited, this miracle must be.

On that splendid day of October 5th 1997, after forty long years of separation, I had a rendezvous with Claudette at two o'clock. I arrived at the restaurant an hour ahead of time as I was so anxious. I was drumming with impatience to finally see her. A thousand questions were set off in my mind, and the only thing to equal my nervousness was my excitement. This hour of waiting seemed an eternity to me. My blood pressure was surely reaching new heights, and I was burning with a strange fever.

My God, may she still find me attractive. Give me the

grace to be able to touch her soul once again and make this fear of false hope within me disappear. . . .

Twenty minutes before the time she was to arrive, I started to doubt whether she would come; had she changed her mind? Had the overpowering emotions of the past made her afraid of rebuilding a relationship with me? Would I be up to her expectations? A torrent of questions rained down upon my spirit . . . When would this torture end?

TWO O'CLOCK at last! Out of the corner of my eye, I catch a shadow sliding by on the restaurant window. Then the VISION: it is a picture of Claudette that draws itself in the door frame, and I reexperience within me the same strong emotion I had felt when we met for the first time in Saint-Placide in 1957! My God, she's so beautiful! She is so ravishing, this woman whom I have always loved! She comes toward me, offers me her hand and disarms me with her most radiant smile . . . I am utterly floored! We sit down together and then, after a troubled silence, we begin to talk, both of us at the same time. She looks at me intensely, astonished and shaken as if she has seen a vision, a ghost from another world. As for me, I am slightly frozen, still too misty to open myself, and it takes all my strength to stifle all the sobs welling up in my throat and the tears that are straining behind my eyes.

Claudette saved me from my embarrassment by taking out of her handbag some photos taken in 1957 and one of the letters I had sent her from Labrador in 1962. The fact that she had kept these souvenirs showed me that she had perhaps not totally forgotten me, and this reassured me a little. As well, I thought I noticed a certain familiar glow in the way that she looked at me, the sweet light of her welcome and the warmth of her whole being had already captured my soul.

I suggested to Claudette that we take a drive to Saint-Placide, that special place where we had first met. On the way we talked to each other, and our hands joined softly in the shyness and decorum of days gone by. We stopped at the house that I had bought on the water's edge and went in. Claudette was overcome with shaking as if she had a premonition that she would return so close to the lake where we fell in love for the first time and where our souls were joined....

The sun was shining, the view was breathtaking. God must have done it on purpose for our reunion! He surrounded us with His most beautiful creations, and He became the accomplice to the reawakening of our sleeping fires. Little by little we recovered our battered senses and decided to go to the village for a walk on the quay that went far out into the blue waters of Lac des Deux-Montagnes. There, seated side by side on a bench, we took in the reflected colors of autumn. The Oka and Rigaud Mountains were mirrored in the calmness of the lake like two handsome rivals. All was silent and serene. We felt no need to talk. Our hearts were joined in thought without our asking. Suddenly Claudette broke the silence: "André, kiss me!"

We had been together for barely two hours when, suddenly and fatefully, our minds came together in the sacred places of our first love. This shared soft kiss was not one of fleeting passion. No, it was the one that joined anew our solitary souls so long apart.

On the way back to Lachute, we already sensed the implacability of our situation. Without openly acknowledging it, we knew that our lives were now unavoidably linked and that nothing in this world would ever be able to keep us apart. Incredible! Our love had been so intense that it had been able to survive forty years of separation! In the course of the weeks that followed, we would meet and go to visit her father at the hospital. I called her as often as I could, to reassure her as to my intentions and to comfort her in her time of trial. She was apprehensive about everything that had happened to us, she thought she was dreaming it all. She still didn't dare to believe in this unexpected happiness. But then we both knew that we were totally powerless before the overwhelming tidal wave that was carrying us to our destiny.

When my wife found out that I had met with Claudette, her anger got the best of her, and life at the house became completely unbearable. I had to leave this living hell sooner than expected in order to avoid scenes that were as disagreeable as they were purposeless. I quickly got my family together to inform my closest relations what I was about to do. The resulting discussion created a shock wave in the family and upset some of those around us, but nothing and no one was able to block the way to our destiny.

In a very short time, Claudette's father's condition worsened. The day he died, she was at his bedside. I shared her pain and sadness and her feelings of fragility in that emotional whirlpool. After the funeral I met her twin daughters, who were greatly astonished by the story of what had happened to us.... One could be surprised by less! We parted and when I got back to the house, my wife told me that she wanted me to move out as soon as possible. Faced with this decision, I had to quickly find somewhere else to live. I called Claudette in Hull and asked her if I should rent a small place while waiting for us to get back together or if she was ready to welcome me right away at her condo. She answered me without a moment's hesitation that I could be with her as soon as I wished and that I didn't have to move elsewhere. On October 30th, twenty-five days after having found the woman of my life again, I moved to Hull to be with the one I loved!

Such is the strength of our love that we can hardly believe it ourselves. Was it a paranormal phenomenon to be able to get back together after forty years still filled with this unspoiled love that could never seem to be completely extinguished? Why could our souls remember the smallest details of our first meeting and the purity of our relationship? Why? These questions without answers enlivened our conversations and added mystery to our marvelous reunion.

A friend of Claudette's lent her a book written on the subject of "twin-soul love" while saying that it might help her to discover something about the kind of love that she was experiencing, The book's authors are experienced researchers in the field of the twin-soul phenomenon; and they have cited many real-life examples that closely resemble the very deep love that Claudette and I enjoy. Upon reading this book, we found undeniable signs, which proved that our souls were meant to meet at the proper time and place in our lives: We were in awe when we discovered that our souls were clearly "twins" and thus forever inseparable!

The theories explained in this marvelous work (entitled "Twin Souls"), are based on actual life situations and provide valuable information on love's great expectations. Here are some of the numerous findings of this research:

Twin-Soul Love

The principle that no human being is really alone, that each individual possesses a "second half" in the opposite sex, is not a new concept, as it has been prevailing for a very long time. The theories of twin soul attraction have always been a preoccupation in the evolution of mankind.

The matching of twin souls happens when two compatible individuals have attained a high level of spiritual realization, so many are disappointed in their love and human relations; but let it be known that it is now possible to find twin-soul models that they can integrate.

In these modern and hectic times, when human and sexual relations are in a confused state, this book is more than timely: its message is unique and spiritually comforting. This inspirational wellspring endows the readers with a new and profound sense of hope and expectation.

From the time of our reuniting on October 5th, we had not stopped marveling at the intensity of our love for each other, and each of our encounters called forth a new display of emotions that we have a hard time controlling.... Claudette wrote down what she was feeling at the time, and her words beautifully describe what her soul was experiencing:

After I saw him

He talked of love, of life,
Of the love of a life,
Of the only love of a life.
It's too close to me;
I can only hear the echo of my heart ;
I can't for the moment
Put words to the dream that lives within me.

Taking a chance on a dream,
Risking heartbreak,
I dream of a love nest
Close to the water, where birds sing,
A haven of harmony
Where goodness guides,
A shelter where smiles
Can smooth the wrinkles of care.
Hands, your hands
Eyes, your eyes
A mouth, your mouth
And words and hymns.

Come and find me.
I await you
Take me
Love me,
From the very first,

I await you.

I have always loved you,
Never scorned.

I always believed in your soul
Despite its folly.

"I adore you next to God
And I will love you forever."
Those words of yours have dwelt
    within my soul.

I know that your pain was deep
And I was not the cause.
I sat powerless to change our destiny,
I saw my dream fade;
I saw the man of my life destroy himself,
I saw his light dim.

Powerless and in shadows
For many years,
I wept as my soul split.
All the tears shed
Made me a river
To float me away
And away, I went.

It was the end of October, and our emotional break-loose left us totally exhausted. We felt the need to slow down the pace, to take some time off, to recover, and to get our strength back. In the hurly-burly of everyday life, we couldn't find the peace and quiet that we needed to address or to take in all the changes that we were encountering. I suggested to Claudette that we take off to Florida for a month in order to fully experience all the joys of our love.

We also had to plan for our future while taking a vacation, if not a well-deserved rest.

In an enchanting spot by the sea, we could finally be alone, far from the intrusive worries of daily existence. There we could look back together on the unfolding of our lives, discover the deep spiritual nature of our love, and take in the all-encompassing reality of the twinning of our souls. All the important decisions were easier to make, as we were in complete harmony. Our happiness was so perfect that nothing concerning the material world took up much room on our scale of values. And it was an easy decision to make our home in Saint-Placide and to sell Claudette's condominium in Hull, to retire fully and so on.

Returning to Hull after a dream vacation, we got the wheels rolling on the plans that we had laid out in Florida. Then too, we thought it might really be interesting to write to the authors of "Twin Souls" and perhaps get their educated opinion about our experience. Also we, Claudette and I, prepared a condensed version of the events in our lives and our experience of reuniting, which we sent off to Dr. Pressman, psychiatrist and co-author of this book that had so impressed us. A few weeks later, we received his answer.

In June 1998 we moved into our dream house in Saint-Placide beside the lake, hardly two hundred yards from the place where we met in 1957 at my parents' cottage! We can see from our window the little bay where I saw Claudette for the first time over forty years ago and where the only true and greatest love of our life was born. The fact of finding this wonderful love intact after all those years is really and truly our "One Last Miracle," which will stay with us as long as we live and will follow us into eternity.

Yes, the downy flakes of spring snow danced to the sound of the church bells of Saint-Pierre-Claver on March 12, 1930 to celebrate my arrival on this earth....

And then, in March 2000, the bells of Saint-Germain d'Outremont rang out for my ninety-four-year-old mother's funeral, my accomplice of all time . . . and the day after her departure, I dedicated my thirty years of sobriety cake to her memory in the warmth and love that only an intimate meeting of Alcoholics Anonymous can provide.

Happiness has no explanation. Claudette and I are content to live it while thanking God, who has never let us down since that wonderful day when I was no longer thirsty. Thank you, God.

Epilogue

In my dream, I am standing precariously on the lookout platform of a lighthouse admiring the pounding surf below... Suddenly there is a rumbling, and the rock beneath the tower starts to crack open and begins to disintegrate. Feelings of fear and vertigo overcome me as I am about to be broken on the rocks below. Then I am startled by a strong voice within me saying: "Fear not, don't stop, jump now!" As the tower sways and the platform gives way beneath me, I jump. I glide slowly through the air and angel-like mermaids cushion my fall into the foaming sea. Gently brought to shore, I find that I am now holding a book in my hands: I open it and discover the story of my life!

The lookout platform in my dream is the stepping stone that leads me to my twin soul at the most painful moment of our solitude.

The "leap of faith" from the platform is absolutely essential to being able to understand the gift of one's inner self-knowledge as depicted by the book in my dream.

All my fears have vanished: they have been replaced by a confidence and an unshakable faith in the strength of a Higher Power that has given me back everything I had lost.

Of all my restored lives, the most rewarding and the most marvelous remains my spiritual life and the return of my twin soul Claudette. This sacred union with her confirms the eternal meaning of our existence and the long lastingness of our love.

Whatever our souls are made of, Claudette's and my own are identical. She is as much me as I can be myself.